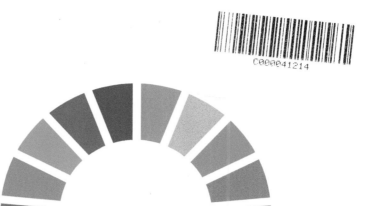

The Sustainable Development Goals Report 2023: Special edition

Towards a Rescue Plan for People and Planet

Foreword

Halfway to the deadline for the 2030 Agenda, the SDG Progress Report; Special Edition shows we are leaving more than half the world behind. Progress on more than 50 per cent of targets of the SDGs is weak and insufficient; on 30 per cent, it has stalled or gone into reverse. These include key targets on poverty, hunger and climate. Unless we act now, the 2030 Agenda could become an epitaph for a world that might have been.

The COVID-19 pandemic and the triple crises of climate change, biodiversity loss and pollution are having a devastating and lasting impact. This has been amplified by Russia's invasion of Ukraine, which has driven increases in the prices of food and energy and in the cost of access to finance, creating a global cost-of-living crisis affecting billions of people.

Developing countries are bearing the brunt of our collective failure to invest in the Sustainable Development Goals (SDGs). Many face a huge financing gap and are buried under a mountain of debt. One in three countries is at high risk of being unable to service their debt.

Developed countries adopted expansionary fiscal and monetary policies during the pandemic and have largely returned to pre-pandemic growth paths. But developing countries were unable to do so, in part because of the risk that their currencies would collapse. Flows of Official Development Assistance are far below the long-standing commitment of 0.7 per cent of GNI. And the financial markets routinely charge developing countries interest rates up to eight times higher than developed countries.

Climate finance is also far below commitments and developed countries have not delivered the $100 billion that was promised annually from 2020.

Meanwhile, vulnerable Middle-Income countries are denied debt relief and concessional financing, and the G20's Common Framework for Debt Treatment is simply not working.

The SDGs are the universally-agreed road map to bridge economic and geopolitical divides, restore trust and rebuild solidarity. Failure to make progress means inequalities will continue to deepen, increasing the risk of a fragmented, two-speed world. No country can afford to see the 2030 Agenda fail.

This report sounds the alarm, calling for a Rescue Plan for People and Planet. I hope the SDG Summit in September will agree to back this Rescue Plan, based on a global alliance for SDG action and acceleration by all stakeholders.

First and foremost, the international community must move forward on our proposed SDG Stimulus, to scale up affordable long-term financing for all countries in need.

The SDG Stimulus has three areas for action: a massive surge in finance for development, enabled by a transformation in the business model of Multilateral Development Banks; a new initiative on debt, under which short-term debt could be exchanged for longer-term instruments at lower interest rates; and the expansion of contingency financing to all countries in need. It can be achieved under the current rules and will enable immediate investments in basic services, clean energy and the digital transition.

But to deal with the root causes of this dire situation, we need deep reform of our outdated, dysfunctional and unfair international financial architecture. We urgently need financial institutions that are fit for purpose; that ensure the benefits of globalization flow to all; and that deliver on their mandate by providing a safety net for all countries in troubled times.

In short, we need a new Bretton Woods moment. Developing countries should have proportionate voice and representation in global decision-making institutions and processes. Economic and financial decisions should prioritize the well-being of people and planet. Governments and the private sector should reorient their economies towards low-carbon, resilient patterns of growth.

This report calls for ambitious national benchmarks to eradicate poverty and reduce inequality, focusing on key areas: expanding social protection and decent jobs; tackling the crisis in education; addressing gender inequality; and improving digital inclusion. These shifts must be supported by strengthened national institutions, greater accountability, effective regulatory frameworks and stronger digital infrastructure and data capacity.

All of this requires strengthened multilateral cooperation and support for the United Nations development system. Most of all, it requires ambitious, decisive, committed action at the SDG Summit in September and the Summit of the Future next year.

We are at a moment of truth and reckoning. But together, we can make this a moment of hope. I urge all Member States to make 2023 the moment when we jump-start progress on the SDGs, to create a more peaceful and prosperous future for all.

António Guterres
Secretary-General of the United Nations

Introduction

We have entered an age of polycrisis. Conflict, climate change, the lingering effects of the COVID-19 pandemic and other global challenges are threatening to derail hard-earned progress towards the SDGs.

While the worst of the COVID-19 pandemic appears to be over, the world is still reeling from its impacts. The recovery has been slow, uneven and incomplete. The pandemic has created significant reversals in global health outcomes. Childhood vaccinations have experienced the largest decline in three decades, and tuberculosis and malaria deaths have increased compared with pre-pandemic levels. COVID-19 has also had devastating impacts on education, causing learning losses in four out of five of the 104 countries studied. Its economic after-effects are equally severe. The pandemic interrupted three decades of steady progress of poverty reduction with the number of people living in extreme poverty increasing for the first time in a generation. It has also caused the largest rise in between-country inequality in three decades.

By May 2023, the devastating consequences of war, conflict and human rights violations had displaced a staggering 110 million people, of which 35 million were refugees – the highest figures ever recorded. Nearly 7,000 people died during migration worldwide in 2022, with the number of deaths in various regions returning to pre-pandemic levels and, in many instances, even surpassing them.

The climate crisis is worsening as greenhouse gas emissions continue to rise. The latest Intergovernmental Panel on Climate Change report finds that global temperature is already 1.1 °C above pre-industrial levels and is likely to reach or surpass the critical 1.5 °C tipping point by 2035. Catastrophic and intensifying heat waves, droughts, flooding and wildfires have become far too frequent. Rising sea levels are threatening hundreds of millions of people in coastal communities. In addition, the world is currently facing the largest species extinction event since the dinosaur age and the oceans were burdened with over 17 million metric tons of plastic pollution in 2021, with projections showing a potential doubling or tripling by 2040.

Developing countries are grappling with an unprecedented rise in external debt following the pandemic, a situation compounded by inflation, rising interest rates, trade tensions and constrained fiscal capacity. Reforms of global governance and of international financial institutions are urgently needed to make them fit for purpose – and fit for the future – by giving more voice and participation to developing countries.

This special edition of the Sustainable Development Goals Report reminds us that there is still much work to be done. Its comprehensive assessment of global progress towards the SDGs paints a sobering picture. Yet, this report also provides a vision of hope by showcasing the progress the world has made so far and the potential for further advancements.

The task ahead is daunting, but it is not impossible. With just seven years left to deliver transformational change, political leaders and public institutions will need to rally all stakeholders around the SDGs and strengthen collaboration, while building trust and accountability. Steps like regulatory innovations that align private sector governance models with sustainable development objectives could spark significant change, if applied soon enough.

The SDG Summit taking place in September will be a critical moment for Member States to galvanize efforts and renew their commitment to the SDGs. It will also be an opportunity for all of us – citizens, civil society, the private sector and other stakeholders – to advocate for urgency, ambition and action to realize the Goals.

The 2030 Agenda remains the clearest blueprint of humanity's highest aspirations. When historians write about the twenty-first century, they will judge leaders and policymakers by whether they have succeeded in transforming this blueprint into reality. Back in September 2015, when global leaders met to adopt the SDGs, they declared that "the future of humanity and of our planet lies in our hands." At this midpoint, these words are truer than ever. It is now up to all of us to ensure that the Sustainable Development Goals are achieved – in full and on time.

LI Junhua
Under-Secretary-General for Economic and Social Affairs

I. Promise in peril

Leave no one behind. That defining principle of the 2030 Agenda for Sustainable Development is a shared promise by every country to work together to secure the rights and well-being of everyone on a healthy, thriving planet. But halfway to 2030, that promise is in peril. The Sustainable Development Goals are disappearing in the rear-view mirror, as is the hope and rights of current and future generations. A fundamental shift is needed – in commitment, solidarity, financing and action – to put the world on a better path. And it is needed now.

We can do better, and in moments of severe challenge, humanity has always come through. Now is another of those moments. The SDG Summit, to be held in September 2023, must signal a genuine turning point. It must mobilize the political commitment and breakthroughs our world desperately needs. It must right the historic injustices at the core of the international financial system to give the most vulnerable countries and people a fair chance at a better future. It must deliver a rescue plan for people and planet.

A. Delivering on commitments: where do we stand halfway to 2030?

Early efforts after the Sustainable Development Goals were adopted produced some favourable trends. Extreme poverty and child mortality rates continued to fall. Inroads were made against such diseases as HIV and hepatitis. Some targets for gender equality were seeing positive results. Electricity access in the poorest countries was on the rise, and the share of renewables in the energy mix was increasing. Globally, unemployment was back to levels not seen since before the 2008 financial crisis. The proportion of waters under national jurisdiction covered by marine protected areas more than doubled in five years. But it is clear now that too much of that progress was fragile and most of it was too slow. In the past three years, the coronavirus disease (COVID-19) pandemic, the war in Ukraine and climate-related disasters have exacerbated already faltering progress.

It is time to sound the alarm. At the midpoint on our way to 2030, the Sustainable Development Goals are in deep trouble. An assessment of the around 140 targets for which trend data is available shows that about half of these targets are moderately or severely off track; and over 30 per cent have either seen no movement or regressed below the 2015 baseline.

Under current trends, 575 million people will still be living in extreme poverty in 2030, and only about one third of countries will meet the target to halve national poverty levels. Shockingly, the world is back at hunger levels not seen since 2005, and food prices remain higher in more countries than in the period 2015–2019. The way things are going, it will take 286 years to close gender gaps in legal protection and remove discriminatory laws. And in education, the impacts of years of underinvestment and learning losses are such that, by 2030, some 84 million children will be out of school and 300 million children or young people attending school will leave unable to read and write.

If ever there was an illumination of the short-sightedness of our prevailing economic and political systems, it is the ratcheting up of the war on nature. A small window of opportunity is fast closing to limit the rise in global temperatures to 1.5 degrees Celsius, prevent the worst impacts of the climate crisis and secure climate justice for people, communities and countries on the front lines of climate change. Carbon dioxide levels continue to rise – to a level not seen in 2 million years. At the current rate of progress, renewable energy sources will continue to account for a mere fraction of our energy supplies in 2030, some 660 million people will remain without electricity, and close to 2 billion people will continue to rely on polluting fuels and technologies for cooking. So much of our lives and health depend on nature, yet it could take another 25 years to halt deforestation, while vast numbers of species worldwide are threatened with extinction.

The lack of progress towards the Sustainable Development Goals is universal, but it is abundantly clear that developing countries and the world's poorest and most vulnerable people are bearing the brunt of our collective failure. This is a direct result of global injustices that go back hundreds of years but are still playing out today. The compounding effects of climate, COVID-19 and economic injustices are leaving many developing countries with fewer options and even fewer resources to make the Goals a reality.

B. Breaking through to a better future for all

We cannot simply continue with more of the same and expect a different result. We cannot persist with a morally bankrupt financial system and expect developing countries to meet targets that developed countries met with far fewer constraints. The 2030 Agenda stated that this generation could be the first to succeed in ending poverty – and the last to have a chance of saving the planet. This higher purpose remains within grasp, but it requires an unprecedented effort by individual Governments, a renewed sense of common purpose across the international community and a global alliance for Sustainable Development Goals-related action across business, civil society, science, young people, local authorities and more. It requires that we come together in September to deliver a rescue plan for people and planet.

Building on the evidence captured in the Global Sustainable Development Report and on the lessons since 2015, the present report identifies a series of urgent actions for your consideration in five key areas.

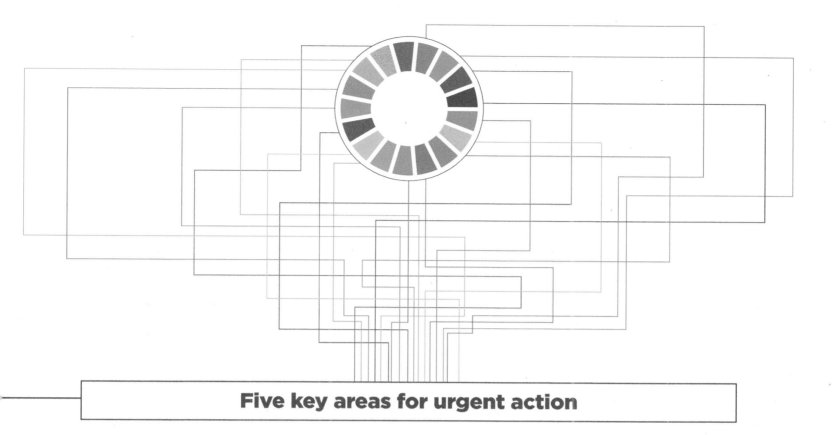

Five key areas for urgent action

1

Heads of State and Government should recommit to seven years of accelerated, sustained and transformative action, both nationally and internationally, to deliver on the promise of the Sustainable Development Goals.

2

Governments should advance concrete, integrated and targeted policies and actions to eradicate poverty, reduce inequality and end the war on nature, with a focus on advancing the rights of women and girls and empowering the most vulnerable.

3

Governments should strengthen national and subnational capacity, accountability and public institutions to deliver accelerated progress towards achieving the Sustainable Development Goals.

4

The international community should recommit at the SDG Summit to deliver on the Addis Ababa Action Agenda and to mobilize the resources and investment needed for developing countries to achieve the Sustainable Development Goals, particularly those in special situations and experiencing acute vulnerability.

5

Member States should facilitate the continued strengthening of the United Nations development system and boost the capacity of the multilateral system to tackle emerging challenges and address Sustainable Development Goals-related gaps and weaknesses in the international architecture that have emerged since 2015.

First, Heads of State and Government should recommit to seven years of accelerated, sustained and transformative action, both nationally and internationally, to deliver on the promise of the Sustainable Development Goals.

This calls for strengthening social cohesion in order to secure dignity, opportunity and rights for all while reorienting economies through green and digital transitions and towards resilient trajectories compatible with the goal of the Paris Agreement to limit the global temperature increase to 1.5 degrees Celsius. It calls for a once-in-a-generation commitment to overhaul the international financial and economic system so that it responds to today's challenges, not those of the 1940s. And it calls for unprecedented collaboration among members of the Group of 20 and support for all developing countries to advance Sustainable Development Goals-related and climate-related action.

Member States should adopt an ambitious and forward-looking political declaration and present global and national commitments for Goals-related transformation at the SDG Summit.

Second, Governments should advance concrete, integrated and targeted policies and actions to eradicate poverty, reduce inequality and end the war on nature, with a focus on advancing the rights of women and girls and empowering the most vulnerable.

This requires the following: giving meaning to the commitment to leave no one behind by expanding social protection floors and access to essential services; creating job opportunities in the care, digital and green economies; urgently tackling the profound crisis in education; strengthening action to advance gender equality, leveraging digital technologies to close divides; supporting the inclusion of persons displaced by crises; and tackling the exclusion of marginalized groups, such as persons with disabilities.

Leaders should embrace the climate acceleration agenda to drive a just renewables revolution and secure climate justice for those on the front lines of the climate crisis. They must also deliver on the Kunming-Montreal Global Biodiversity Framework, work to further reduce risks from disasters and build integrated and sustainable food, water and sanitation systems while making the right to a healthy environment a reality for all people.

Third, Governments should strengthen national and subnational capacity, accountability and public institutions to deliver accelerated progress towards achieving the Sustainable Development Goals.

Delivery of the Sustainable Development Goals must become a central focus for national planning, oversight mechanisms and domestic budgets. Major investments are needed to strengthen public sector capacity and build appropriate digital infrastructure. Local and subnational governments must be empowered and supported to bring implementation of the Goals to the ground level. An effective regulatory framework is needed to align private sector governance models with sustainable development objectives. A fresh push is needed to reap the data dividend, and the monitoring, follow-up and review of the Goals must be taken to the next level, including by strengthening civic space and public engagement in policy- and decision-making.

Fourth, to ensure that developing countries can deliver in these areas, the international community should recommit at the SDG Summit to deliver on the Addis Ababa Action Agenda and to mobilize the resources and investment needed for developing countries to achieve the Sustainable Development Goals, particularly those in special situations and experiencing acute vulnerability.

Member States should endorse and deliver a $500 billion per year Sustainable Development Goals stimulus plan between now and 2030.

This calls for immediate action: (a) to tackle the high cost of debt and the rising risks of debt distress, including by converting short-term, high-interest borrowing into long-term (more than 30 year) debt at lower interest rates; (b) to massively scale-up affordable, long-term financing for development, especially through multilateral development banks, rechannelling special drawing rights and aligning all financing flows with the Goals; and (c) to expand contingency financing to all countries in need.

Member States should recognize and address the need for deep reforms of the international financial architecture through a new Bretton Woods moment, including by enhancing the voice and participation of developing countries in the governance of international financial institutions. This is essential in order to ensure that the financial architecture delivers for all developing countries and secures urgent access to grants and long-term concessional finance as they transition to renewable energy-based, climate-resilient, inclusive economies. It requires building on the lessons from recent efforts to mobilize private finance, including revising risk appetite and the criteria used by credit ratings agencies and adjusting policies and instruments.

Finally, Member States should facilitate the continued strengthening of the United Nations development system and boost the capacity of the multilateral system to tackle emerging challenges and address Sustainable Development Goals-related gaps and weaknesses in the international architecture that have emerged since 2015.

The United Nations development system continues to play a crucial role in supporting countries in delivering on their national Goals-related ambitions. What the system offers has evolved considerably since 2015, enabled by the most ambitious reforms in decades. The UN system will continue to strengthen its offer. Member States should continue to support the contribution of Resident Coordinators and United Nations country teams by delivering on the funding compact, ensuring the resident coordinator system is fully funded and further capitalizing the Joint Sustainable Development Goals Fund.

Many of the proposals in Our Common Agenda are already supporting acceleration towards achieving the Goals. Member States, through the forthcoming Summit of the Future, should build on the commitment and direction provided by the SDG Summit to ensure progress in other areas of particular importance for Goals-related progress. Those areas include reforming the international architecture, going beyond gross domestic product (GDP), strengthening digital cooperation, boosting youth participation in decision-making, transforming education, establishing an emergency platform and advancing a new agenda for peace. Further action is also needed to boost the capacities of developing countries in the areas of trade and technology, to align global trading rules with the Sustainable Development Goals and to establish more efficient and effective technology transfer mechanisms.

History has shown that the worst hardships can be overcome through human determination, solidarity, leadership and resilience. The destruction brought about by World War II was followed by new forms of solidarity and cooperation through the United Nations and the Marshall Plan. This period also witnessed advances in global positioning systems, modern air travel and satellite communications, as well as accelerated decolonization. Preventing widespread hunger and starvation in the 1960s galvanized investment in agriculture and the green revolution. Other more recent examples include the global responses to fight HIV/AIDS and, in part, the surge in action and community to save lives and livelihoods during the COVID-19 pandemic.

These outcomes, by no means inevitable, resulted from unique combinations of purpose, solidarity, ingenuity and technology. This moment of peril demands a similar response if we are to deliver on our 2015 promise.

II. Sounding the alarm: Sustainable Development Goals progress at the midpoint

At the midpoint of the implementation of the 2030 Agenda, a sobering reality emerges: the world is falling short of meeting most of the Goals by 2030. While certain areas have witnessed progress, there remains a concerning proportion of targets that are either progressing too slowly or regressing.

This section of the report provides a comprehensive overview of progress under each goal and offers a candid assessment based on the latest available data and estimates from more than 50 international agencies. Through an examination of selected targets under each goal, we uncover both successes and challenges, bringing attention to areas requiring urgent attention. This assessment compels us to acknowledge the existing gaps and calls for a redoubling of efforts on a global scale.

Moreover, this section highlights the remarkable advancements in data availability for SDG indicators and proactive measures taken by the data and statistical community, showcasing the progress made over time. It underscores the vital role of investing in data for accelerating SDG progress. By harnessing the power of data, we can gain valuable insights and drive effective actions towards realizing the 2030 Agenda.

A. Taking stock of SDG progress at the midpoint

A reality check of the progress made on the SDGs at the midpoint towards 2030 reveals significant challenges. The latest global-level data and assessments from custodian agencies[1] paint a concerning picture: of the approximately 140 targets that can be evaluated, half of them show moderate or severe deviations from the desired trajectory. Furthermore, more than 30 per cent of these targets have experienced no progress or, even worse, regression below the 2015 baseline. This assessment underscores the urgent need for intensified efforts to ensure the SDGs stay on course and progress towards a sustainable future for all.

Progress assessment for the 17 Goals based on assessed targets, 2023 or latest data (percentage)

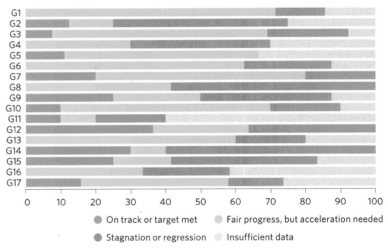

B. Unfolding a remarkable journey of SDG data and monitoring

Despite the challenges in securing timely data across all 169 targets, considerable progress has been achieved in the availability of internationally comparable data: the number of indicators included in the global SDG database has increased from 115 in 2016 to 225 in 2023. The number of data records in the database has increased from 330, 000 in 2016 to 2.7 million as of May 2023. In just seven years, the global SDG database has expanded significantly.

Significant strides have also been made in the methodological development of the SDG indicators as well. In 2016, a concerning 39 per cent of the SDG indicators lacked internationally established methodology or standards. By March 2020, all indicators had a well-established and internationally agreed methodology, which ensure the comparability, accuracy, reliability, and usefulness of our measurements. Continuous refinement and harmonization of methodologies have made the indicator framework more robust. These advancements in methodology provide a solid foundation for monitoring the performance of the SDGs. Moreover, the proportion of indicators that are conceptually clear and have good country coverage has increased significantly from 36 per cent in 2016 to 66 per cent in 2022.

Proportion of global SDG indicators, by availability of standards and national data, 2016-2022 (percentage)

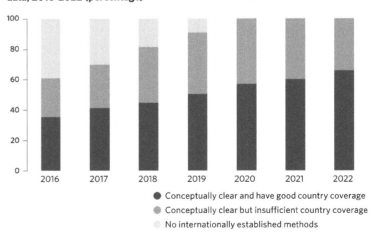

---

[1]   The Global and regional data and assessments for all targets and indicators for which information is available can be found in the Statistical Annex at https://unstats.un.org/sdgs/.

While these achievements are worthy of celebration, we cannot ignore the persistent gaps that still challenge our data landscape. Geographic coverage, timeliness, and disaggregation remain areas of concern. For several cross-cutting goals such as climate action (Goal 13), gender equality (Goal 5), and peace, justice, and strong institutions (Goal 16), less than half of the 193 countries or areas have internationally comparable data since 2015. This stark reality serves as a reminder that we must prioritize gathering essential information on these critical issues that profoundly impact our future and our planet. Furthermore, a significant challenge lies in the timeliness of data, with less than 30 per cent of the latest available data from 2022 and 2023, while over half of the latest data comes from 2020 and 2021. As we embark on delivering a rescue plan for people and planet at the SDG Summit, accelerated action for data is imperative.

National statistical offices are increasingly playing a coordination role, but challenges persist

Empowered by the SDG data requirements, many national statistical offices (NSOs) have taken a bigger coordination or stewardship role within their national statistical systems. In Cambodia, the National Institute of Statistics was mandated by the new statistics law enacted in 2022 to lead statistical data collection and analysis in the country. Similarly, the Philippine Statistics Authority was designated as the official repository of the SDG indicators in the country through a resolution passed in 2016, highlighting their important role in monitoring and reporting on SDG progress.

In Finland, Malaysia and Uganda, the NSOs are leading the national technical working group on SDG data, by providing advice on methodology and ensuring the quality of data from various sources. In the United Kingdom, the Office for National Statistics was actively involved in the 2019 Voluntary National Review from the onset of the process, by supporting a "data-led" reporting and including a dedicated data chapter within the report.

Despite all efforts, challenges remain in the coordination capacity of NSOs within the National Statistical System. A survey conducted in 2021 on the implementation of the Cape Town Global Action Plan for Sustainable Development Data showed that around 53 per cent of the NSOs expressed dissatisfaction with their coordination role. Particularly, in low- and lower-middle income countries, as many as 74 per cent of NSOs felt a need for improvement. Inadequate institutional mechanisms, ineffective communication channels for information sharing, and lack of incentives were identified as the top three challenges impeding better coordination.

Coordination capacity of the NSO with partners inside of the National Statistical System, July 2021 (percentage)

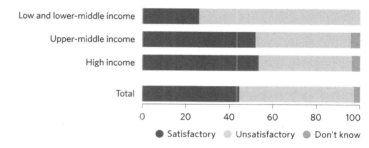

The data demand for the 2030 Agenda has unleashed innovation

The unprecedented data demand driven by the 2030 Agenda has acted as a catalyst for data innovation. For example, household surveys, a longstanding data source, are now embracing modern technologies and inclusive approaches, such as using telephone and web data collection methods to make them more efficient and inclusive. Engaging respondents as co-creators, empowering them to contribute to the data collection process, has further enhanced the quality and relevance of the obtained information. Meanwhile, nontraditional data sources such as administrative records, satellite imagery, and citizen-generated data have emerged as valuable sources in bridging data gaps. Another important aspect of innovation focuses on the integration of multiple data sources.

Tanzania's Statistical Master Plan for 2022–2026 exemplifies this innovative mindset, prioritizing the strengthening of administrative data sources from line ministries and embracing data from non-State actors. Colombia has harnessed the power of satellite imagery to monitor SDG indicators, such as all-season road accessibility, which traditional data sources fail to measure properly. Kenya has incorporated citizen-generated data into its national Data Quality Assurance Framework, which outlines principles and processes for ensuring data quality in SDG monitoring. Meanwhile, Ghana has repurposed data from civil society organizations to inform policies on marine litter, helping shape coastal and marine management policies in the country.

Timeliness and disaggregation are vital components of data production, often necessitating the integration of multiple data sources. Bangladesh, with the support of the Data for Now project, has successfully generated poverty estimates for smaller geographical areas by integrating satellite imagery with household survey data. This innovative approach, known as "small area estimation", is gaining traction in measuring various SDG indicators related to social protection, health, education and employment. Embracing better data integration and interoperability has also prompted concerted efforts to build data partnerships and enhance policy coherence across government entities.

With more recognition of the importance of innovation, continued support is essential. Nearly 90 per cent of NSOs identified the use of administrative data as a high priority for capacity building. Additionally, approximately 50 per cent of NSOs have expressed interest in harnessing the potential of earth observation/satellite imagery and web-based data collection methods.

Capacity-building priorities identified by national statistical offices, July 2021 (percentage)

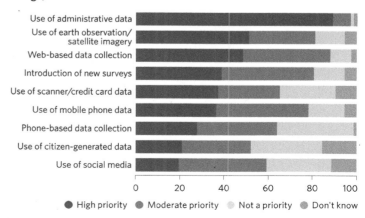

Important partnerships are being established for better and more inclusive data for development

Recognizing the diverse national capacities in data and statistics, countries agree on the importance of adopting a "whole-of-society" approach to meet the monitoring needs of the ambitious 2030 Agenda. The SDG indicator framework has encouraged NSOs to establish partnerships, both within and outside the national statistical system, at national and international levels.

Within governments, the alignment of the global SDG indicator framework with national policy priorities has fostered collaborative efforts between national statistical offices and line ministries. In Cameroon, Mozambique and Uganda, regular stakeholder meetings on SDG data are organized to review and validate national and subnational SDG reports. Brazil has established a National Commission for the SDGs, involving various stakeholders and the country NSO to develop data action plans for each of the 17 Goals. The United Kingdom's 2019 VNR process saw the participation of over 380 organizations, highlighting a commitment to inclusivity.

The public sector has been the main partner of national statistical offices, with 80 per cent of NSOs having institutional arrangements with other government entities. Collaboration with international organizations is also common, with 66 per cent of countries reporting such partnerships. Additionally, academia, the private sector, and civil society organizations have emerged as important partners for NSOs. However, 13 per cent of countries indicated a lack of arrangements with other stakeholders. Moving forward, it is crucial to make efforts in building partnerships with a wide range of stakeholders to further strengthen data monitoring efforts for the SDGs.

At the international level, the SDG monitoring process has also sparked collaboration among diverse stakeholders. The Inter-Agency and Expert Group on SDG Indicators, responsible for the development and implementation of the global indicator framework for the SDGs, has been instrumental in fostering collaboration among stakeholders from different data communities at local, national, regional, and international levels.

Proportion of national statistical offices with institutional arrangement with stakeholders (percentage)

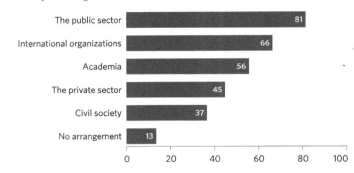

Programmes such as the SDG16 Survey Initiative have advanced methodologies for areas where official statistics were previously lacking, including discrimination and government transparency. The Collaborative on the Use of Administrative Data facilitates the sharing of tools and experiences to support countries in utilizing administrative data for statistical purposes. Members of the Inter-Secretariat Working Group on Household Surveys collaborate to provide coordinated support to countries on survey activities. Furthermore, the recently launched Collaborative on Citizen Contributions to Data, mandated by the Statistical Commission, aims to strengthen the capacity of NSOs, academia and civil society organizations in leveraging citizen data for the SDGs. Through these international collaborations, innovative approaches and best practices are being shared, empowering countries to overcome data challenges and enhance their data capabilities.

Increased openness, accessibility and effective use of data have helped achieve better data impact

The increased openness, accessibility, and effective use of data have played a crucial role in achieving better data impact. Since the adoption of the 2030 Agenda, significant progress has been made by countries in opening up official statistics. According to the Open Data Watch, the median score of data openness among 165 countries increased from 38 in 2016 to 57 in 2022. However, a mean score of 57 out of 100 clearly highlights the need for further efforts to enhance data openness. One key step in adding value to existing data collection is the dissemination of microdata, which allows researchers to conduct more in-depth analysis, promotes transparency and accountability, and fosters collaboration. Only less than half of the low- and lower-middle income countries disseminate survey microdata data through national repositories.

Data plays a pivotal role in shaping policies and driving meaningful change. In Chile, for instance, poverty estimates derived from integrating data from administrative sources and household surveys have informed the allocation of funds to all municipalities. In Moldova, data collected from the Household Budget Survey played a vital role in enabling the government to provide credit to households affected by the energy crisis. The Gambia's national SDG 16 survey, which measures citizens' satisfaction with government services, led to the establishment of a new ministry overseeing public service delivery by the newly elected President. Citizen-generated data, through its citizen-led approach, has also played a significant role in advancing progress on Goal 16, contributing to more inclusive societies and sustainable development.

Investing in better data is key to supporting a rescue plan for people and planet

The need for data capacity building has never been so urgent, as countries face multiple crises on health, food, energy and climate, and need better data to support policymaking. It is also paramount to ensure effective monitoring and reporting on the progress towards achieving the SDGs.

However, NSOs are facing significant funding gap, particularly in low and middle-income countries. Approximately 23 per cent of NSOs in low and lower-middle income countries are experiencing severe funding shortages, with funding gaps exceeding 60 per cent for their statistical programmes. About 50 per cent of NSOs in this group face moderate funding gaps ranging from 20 to 60 per cent. The situation is relatively better for upper-middle-income countries, with around 13 per cent facing severe funding shortages and 50 per cent experiencing moderate levels of funding gaps. These funding challenges pose a significant hurdle to building strong data capacities and hinder effective monitoring and reporting on SDG progress.

In response to the funding gap in data, the recently launched Hangzhou declaration "Accelerating progress in the implementation of the Cape Town Global Action Plan for Sustainable Development Data", called for "an urgent and sustained increase in the level and scale of investments in data and statistics from domestic and international actors, from the public, private

and philanthropic sectors, to strengthen statistical capacity in low-income countries and fragile states, close data gaps for vulnerable groups and enhance country resilience in the current context of economic crisis, conflict, climate change and increased food insecurity."

Funding gap for national statistical offices' work programme, by income level, July 2021 (percentage)

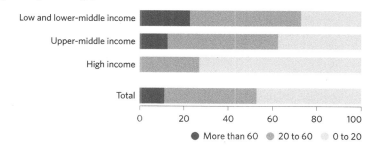

SDG PROGRESS UNVEILED: A DATA JOURNEY

A CONCERNING PICTURE OF SDG PROGRESS AT THE MIDPOINT:

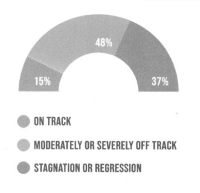

- ● ON TRACK
- ● MODERATELY OR SEVERELY OFF TRACK
- ● STAGNATION OR REGRESSION

BASED ON AN ASSESSMENT OF SDG TARGETS WITH TREND DATA.

SIGNIFICANT STRIDES IN SDG DATA AND MONITORING

INDICATORS WITH INTERNATIONALLY AGREED METHODOLOGY

DATA RECORDS IN SDG GLOBAL DATABASE

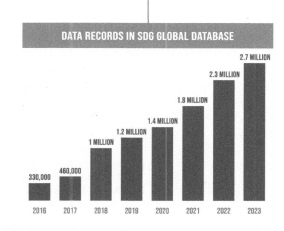

MIND THE GAP FOR BETTER DATA

NATIONAL STATISTICAL OFFICES SATISFIED WITH THEIR COORDINATION ROLE

  54% HIGH-INCOME  **26%** LOW- AND LOWER-MIDDLE INCOME

COUNTRIES WITH >60% FUNDING GAP IN THEIR STATISTICAL PROGRAMME

  0% HIGH-INCOME **23%** LOW- AND LOWER-MIDDLE INCOME

No poverty

Daily life of residents living in the Sujat Nagar slum in Dhaka, Bangladesh.

- If current trends continue, 575 million people will still be living in extreme poverty and only one-third of countries will have halved their national poverty levels by 2030.

- Despite the expansion of social protection during the COVID-19 crisis, over 4 billion people remain entirely unprotected. Many of the world's vulnerable population groups, including the young and the elderly, remain uncovered by statutory social protection programmes.

- The share of government spending on essential services, such as education, health and social protection, is significantly higher in advanced economies than in emerging and developing economies.

- A surge in action and investment to enhance economic opportunities, improve education and extend social protection to all, particularly the most excluded, is crucial to delivering on the central commitment to end poverty and leave no one behind.

Slow and uneven progress on poverty reduction may leave hundreds of millions in extreme poverty by 2030

Extreme poverty, currently defined as living on less than $2.15 per person per day at 2017 purchasing power parity, had experienced a significant decline in recent decades. However, COVID-19 reversed this positive trend. Even before the pandemic, the pace of poverty reduction was slowing, with extreme poverty falling from 10.8 per cent in 2015 to 8.4 per cent in 2019. The average annual reduction rate was 0.54 percentage points between 2015 and 2019, less than half the 1.28 percentage-point rate observed between 2000 and 2014. In 2020, the number of people living in extreme poverty rose to 724 million, surpassing the pre-pandemic projection by 90 million and reversing approximately three years of progress on poverty reduction.

Recovery from the pandemic has been slow and uneven, with extreme poverty dropping from 9.3 per cent in 2020 to 8.8 per cent in 2021. About 41 per cent of low-income countries experienced a higher poverty rate in 2021 compared to the previous year, versus only 13 per cent of upper-middle-income countries. The conflict in Ukraine has disrupted global trade, leading to increased living costs that are disproportionately impacting the poor. Furthermore, climate change poses substantial threats to poverty reduction. By the end of 2022, nowcasting suggests that 8.4 per cent of the world's population, or as many as 670 million people, could still be living in extreme poverty.

If current trends continue, an estimated 7 per cent of the global population – approximately 575 million people – will still be living in extreme poverty by 2030, with most in sub-Saharan Africa. This projection would represent a meager poverty reduction of less than 30 per cent since 2015.

Proportion of the world's population living below $2.15/day, 2015–2019 realized and 2020–2030 forecast and projected (percentage)

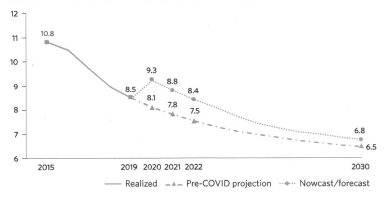

If current trends continue, only one third of countries will halve national poverty by 2030

The national poverty line is a measure that is specific to a country's economic conditions that can help policymakers design targeted interventions and social safety nets. In 2020, 22 out of 39 countries with data saw increases in national poverty rates relative to the previous year. Given the historical trends of 127 countries with data, only one third of countries will have halved their national poverty rates by 2030 from 2015.

Poverty is a complex and multidimensional challenge. Some countries have also adopted national multidimensional poverty indicators to capture other aspects of poverty – such as those related to health, employment, education and access to basic services – as well as to reveal the interconnections between deprivations across multiple Goals within households. Despite the implementation of these measures in a few countries, progress on reducing national multidimensional poverty has been limited. To address this, governments and stakeholders must target underlying factors and develop strategies to alleviate deprivations across multiple dimensions.

Amid overlapping crises, coverage and expenditures on social protection programmes remain low

The COVID-19 pandemic has highlighted the importance of social protection systems. However, in 2020, a mere 47 per cent of the global population was effectively covered by at least one social protection cash benefit, a slight increase from 45 per cent in 2015. Only 26.4 per cent of children under the age of 15 worldwide received social protection cash benefits, compared with 77.5 per cent of older persons. However, in low-income countries, only 23.2 per cent of older persons of pensionable age received social protection cash benefits. Similarly, globally, only 28.9 per cent of people considered vulnerable – all children, along with adults and older people not covered by contributory programmes – had access to non-contributory cash benefits.

Moreover, national expenditures on social protection for children and the elderly remain low, with upper-middle-income countries spending just 0.5 per cent and 1.4 per cent of GDP, and lower-middle-income countries spending 0.1 per cent and 0.8 per cent of GDP, respectively, in 2020. In response to the cost-of-living crisis, 105 countries and territories announced almost 350 social protection measures between February 2022 and February 2023. However, more than 80 per cent of these measures were short term in nature and around 47 per cent were general income support for the poor and vulnerable, particularly children, families and the elderly

population. To achieve the Goals, countries will need to implement nationally appropriate universal and sustainble social protection systems for all.

Proportion of children, vulnerable persons and older persons covered by social protection cash benefits, by income level of country, 2020 (percentage)

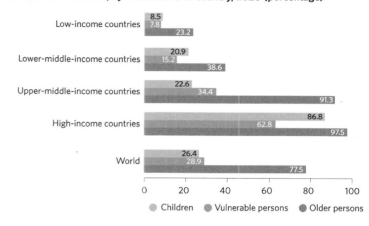

Advanced, emerging and developing economies alike have all increased their share of government spending on essential services

The share of government spending on essential services, including education, health and social protection, has increased over the past two decades. It accounted for approximately 53 per cent of total government expenditures globally in 2021, a rise from 47 per cent in 2015. This figure reached 62 per cent in advanced economies and 44 per cent in emerging and developing economies. The gap between them has remained relatively stable, at approximately 20 percentage points over the years. Looking into

the different components of essential services, social protection spending in advanced economies was on average 17 percentage points higher than in emerging and developing economies, in part reflecting higher pension coverage in the former. The gap was lower when it comes to health spending, which was 6 percentage points higher on average in advanced economies compared to emerging and developing economies.

Globally, disasters are affecting more people but causing fewer deaths

At the mid-point of the 2030 Agenda for Sustainable Development and the Sendai Framework for Disaster Risk Reduction, there has been a progressive decline in disaster-related mortality. The global average annual number of deaths or missing persons per 100,000 population has steadily decreased worldwide, from 1.64 in the period of 2005–2015 to 0.86 in 2012–2021. In absolute terms, countries reported an average disaster mortality of 44,616 per year during this period. However, least developed countries (LDCs), small island developing States (SIDS) and landlocked developing countries (LLDCs) face higher vulnerability to disasters, with mortality rates of 1.24, 2.80 and 1.85, respectively, from 2012–2021. Despite the decline in global disaster-related mortality, the number of people affected by disasters per 100,000 population has increased from 1,198 during 2005–2015 to 2,113 in the 2012–2021 period (excluding cases related to COVID-19). Between 2015 and 2021, a staggering 151 million people on average were affected by disasters each year globally.

Disaster-related mortality rate (excluding COVID-19 deaths), 2005–2021 (deaths per 100,000 population)

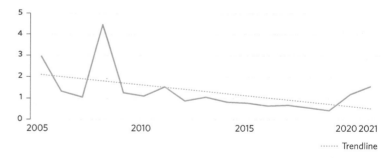

Zero hunger

- The number of people facing hunger and food insecurity has been rising since 2015, with the pandemic, conflict, climate change and growing inequalities exacerbating the situation. In 2022, about 9.2 per cent of the world population was facing chronic hunger, equivalent to about 735 million people – 122 million more than in 2019. An estimated 29.6 per cent of the global population – 2.4 billion people – were moderately or severely food insecure, meaning they did not have access to adequate food. This figure reflects an alarming 391 million more people than in 2019.

- Despite global efforts, in 2022, an estimated 45 million children under the age of 5 suffered from wasting, 148 million had stunted growth and 37 million were overweight. A fundamental shift in trajectory is needed to achieve the 2030 nutrition targets.

- To achieve zero hunger by 2030, urgent coordinated action and policy solutions are imperative to address entrenched inequalities, transform

Children in the Santeng community of Tongo District, Ghana, enjoy porridge made from *fonio*, an ancient indigenous drought-resistant crop cultivated by rural women.

food systems, invest in sustainable agricultural practices, and reduce and mitigate the impact of conflict and the pandemic on global nutrition and food security.

In the face of a polycrisis, joint global efforts are urgently needed to address hunger and ensure food security

In 2022, the prevalence of undernourishment remained unchanged compared to 2021, following a significant increase in 2020 due to the pandemic and a slower rise in 2021. The global population facing chronic hunger stood at 9.2 per cent in 2022, up from 7.9 per cent in 2019, affecting around 735 million people, which is a rise of 122 million since 2019. Moreover, an estimated 2.4 billion individuals, equivalent to 29.6 per cent of the world's population, experienced moderate to severe food insecurity, meaning they did not have regular access to adequate food. While Africa has a higher proportion of its population facing hunger compared to other regions, Asia is home to the majority of people facing hunger. It is projected that more than 600 million people worldwide will be facing hunger in 2030, highlighting the immense challenge of achieving the zero hunger target.

Global trends in the prevalence of hunger and food security reflect the interplay of two opposing forces. On one hand, the resumption of economic activity has led to increased incomes and improved access to food. On the other hand, food price inflation has eroded income gains and hindered access to food. However, these forces have manifested differently across different regions. Hunger continues to increase in Western Asia, the Caribbean, and all subregions of Africa. Conversely, most subregions in Asia and Latin America have experienced improvements in food security.

Prevalence of undernourishment, 2020–2022 average (percentage)

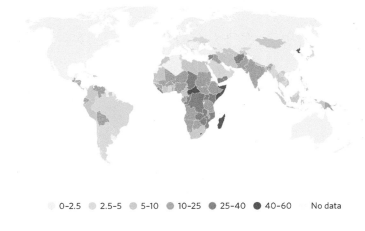

0–2.5   2.5–5   5–10   10–25   25–40   40–60   No data

Aid and public spending on agriculture are falling despite the growing global food crisis

Investment in agriculture is crucial for improving efficiency, productivity and income growth, and for addressing poverty and hunger. Despite record-high nominal public spending on agriculture of $700 billion in 2021 during the pandemic, government expenditures on agriculture relative to the sector's contribution to GDP (as measured by the agriculture orientation index – AOI) fell from a value of 0.50 in 2015 to 0.45 in 2021. This decline was observed in all regions except Europe and Northern America, where stimulus packages of unprecedented scale were implemented by governments. Latin America and the Caribbean recorded the highest decline in AOI, from 0.33 in 2015 to 0.21 in 2021.

Between 2015 and 2021, the total aid to agriculture in developing countries increased by 14.6 per cent, from $12.8 to $14.2 billion (in constant 2021 prices). In 2020, total aid to agriculture spiked, growing by nearly 18 per cent compared to the previous year, partly due to food security concerns during the pandemic. However, in 2021, it fell by 15 per cent, returning to levels similar to those before the pandemic.

Malnutrition continues to threaten children and women worldwide, despite some progress

Children affected by malnutrition – including stunting (low height for age), wasting (low weight for height), micronutrient deficiencies, and by being overweight – face heightened risks of poor growth and development. Despite progress in certain regions, child malnutrition remains a global concern that has been exacerbated by the ongoing food and nutrition crisis – with low- and lower-middle-income countries among those most affected.

In 2022, 22.3 per cent of children under age 5 (148 million) were affected by stunting, down from 26.3 per cent in 2012. While the number of countries with a high prevalence of stunting (30 per cent or more) decreased from 47 to 28 countries from 2012 to 2022, no region is on track to achieve the 2030 target of a 50 per cent reduction in the number of stunted children. If current trends persist, approximately 128.5 million children will still suffer from stunting in 2030. To meet the global target, the annual rate of reduction must increase by 2.2 times the current rate.

Wasting, caused by diseases and nutrient-poor diets, puts children at immediate risk of thinness, weakened immunity, developmental delays and death. In 2022, 6.8 per cent (or 45 million) children under age 5 were affected by wasting, down form 7.7 per cent in 2010. At the same time, 5.6 per cent (or 37 million) were overweight. The global prevalence of overweight children has stagnated at around 5.5 per cent since 2012, requiring greater efforts to achieve the 2030 target of 3 per cent.

Moreover, the prevalence of anaemia in women aged 15–49 continues to be alarming, stagnating at around 30 per cent since 2000. Anaemia in women is a risk factor for adverse maternal and perinatal outcomes, highlighting the importance of addressing this issue for both women and child health and nutrition.

Preventing all forms of malnutrition requires: ensuring adequate maternal nutrition; promoting optimal breastfeeding; providing nutritious, diverse and safe foods in early childhood; and creating a healthy environment, with access to basic health, water, hygiene and sanitation services, as well as opportunities for safe physical activity. Coordinated actions across nutrition, health and social protection sectors – especially in the regions most affected – are needed to reduce child and maternal malnutrition.

Number of children under age 5 who are affected by stunting, 2012 and 2022 (millions)

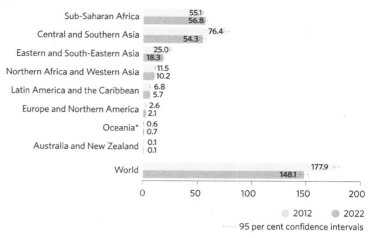

Proportion of children under age 5 who are overweight, 2012 and 2022 (percentage)

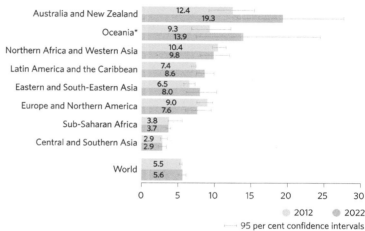

* Excluding Australia and New Zealand.

Despite dropping in 2021, the share of countries experiencing high food prices remained above the 2015–2019 average

Globally, the share of countries experiencing moderately to abnormally high food prices fell from 48.1 per cent in 2020 to 21.5 per cent in 2021. Despite this significant drop, the 2021 figure was still higher than the 2015–2019 average of 15.2 per cent. Factors such as increased demand, rising input (energy and fertilizer) and transport costs, supply chain disruptions and trade policy changes contributed to the sustained price increases. Meanwhile, domestic factors – including adverse weather, currency depreciations, political instability and production shortfalls – intensified price pressures. In sub-Saharan Africa and the least developed countries (LDCs), the proportion of countries experiencing high food prices increased for the second consecutive year in 2021 (reaching 40.9 per cent and 34.1 per cent, respectively). These regions faced additional challenges from worsening security conditions, macroeconomic difficulties, and a high level of dependency on imported food and agricultural inputs.

Proportion of countries affected by moderately to abnormally high food prices, 2015–2019 average, 2020 and 2021 (percentage)

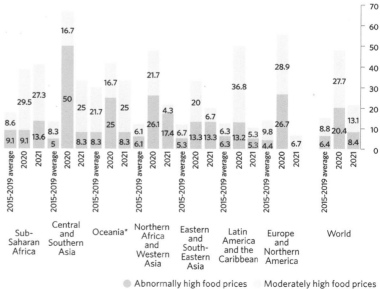

*Excluding Australia and New Zealand.

3 GOOD HEALTH AND WELL-BEING

Good health and well-being

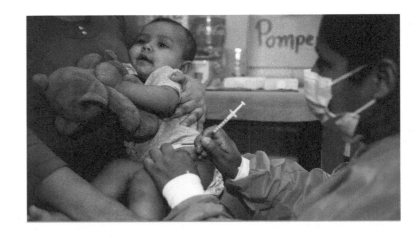

- There has been some progress on improving global health in recent years. For example, 146 out of 200 countries or areas have already met or are on track to meet the SDG target on under-5 mortality. Effective HIV treatment has cut global AIDS-related deaths by 52 per cent since 2010 and at least one neglected tropical disease has been eliminated in 47 countries.

- However, insufficient progress has been made in other areas, such as on reducing maternal mortality and expanding universal health coverage. Globally, approximately 800 women died every day from pregnancy or childbirth in 2020. And 381 million people were pushed or further pushed into extreme poverty in 2019 due to out-of-pocket payments for health.

- The COVID-19 pandemic and ongoing crises have impeded progress towards Goal 3. Childhood vaccinations have experienced the largest decline in three decades, and tuberculosis and malaria deaths have increased compared with pre-pandemic levels.

Nine-month-old Sofia receives routine vaccinations and a medical check-up with her mother at a clinic in Bolivia.

- To overcome these setbacks and address long-standing health care shortcomings, increased investment in health systems is needed to support countries in their recovery and build resilience against future health threats.

Stagnating progress in reducing maternal mortality means a woman dies of preventable causes every two minutes

The global maternal mortality ratio (MMR) marginally declined from 227 deaths per 100,000 live births in 2015 to 223 in 2020. This figure remains over three times the target of 70 set for 2030 – meaning that approximately 800 women died every day from preventable causes related to pregnancy and childbirth, or one death every two minutes. From 2016–2020, the global average annual reduction rate was approximately zero, significantly lower than the 2.7 per cent rate achieved between 2000 and 2015.

In 2020, about 70 per cent maternal deaths occured in sub-Saharan Africa, followed by Central and Southern Asia at nearly 17 per cent. Fifteen-year-old girls in sub-Saharan Africa had the highest lifetime risk (1 in 40) – approximately 400 times higher than their peers in Australia and New Zealand. Between 2016 and 2020, LDCs and LLDCs saw significant drops in MMR, with an average annual reduction rate of 2.8 per cent and 3.0 per cent, respectively, while in SIDS, the annual reduction rate was only 1.2 per cent.

Global coverage of assisted childbirth by skilled health personnel has risen from 81 to 86 per cent between 2015 and 2022, but access remains limited in many countries, particularly in sub-Saharan Africa and Southern Asia, where mortality rates are highest. However, sub-Saharan Africa experienced the fastest growth, from 59 to 70 per cent between 2015 and 2022.

Proportion of births attended by skilled health personnel, 2015 and 2022 (percentage)

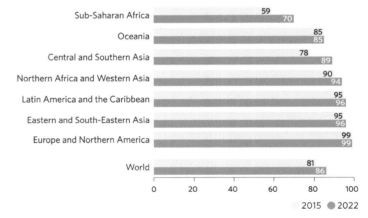

Region	2015	2022
Sub-Saharan Africa	59	70
Oceania	85	85
Central and Southern Asia	78	89
Northern Africa and Western Asia	90	94
Latin America and the Caribbean	95	96
Eastern and South-Eastern Asia	95	96
Europe and Northern America	99	99
World	81	86

● 2015 ● 2022

Progress on reproductive health continues, with falling adolescent birth rates and rising access to contraception

More women and girls now have improved access to sexual and reproductive health services. The proportion of women of reproductive age (15–49 years) having their need for family planning satisfied with modern methods has increased slightly, from 76.5 to 77.6 per cent between 2015 and 2023, and is projected to reach 78.2 per cent by 2030. Sub-Saharan Africa has witnessed the largest increase, from 51.6 to 57.4 per cent during this period, and is expected to rise to 62.1 per cent by 2030.

The global adolescent birth rate for girls aged 15–19 was 41.3 births per 1,000 girls in 2023, down from 47.2 in 2015. The global adolescent birth rate for girls aged 10–14, reported for the first time in the global monitoring of the Goals, has also declined from 1.8 births per 1,000 girls in 2015 to 1.5 in 2023. Latin America and the Caribbean reported the largest reduction, from 67.3 births per 1,000 girls aged 15–19 in 2015 to 51.4 in 2023, and from 3.3 births per 1,000 girls aged 10–14 in 2015 to 2.3 in 2023.

Global child mortality rates show significant decline, but challenges remain

A significant reduction in child mortality has been achieved over the past two decades. Between 2015 and 2021, the global under-5 mortality rate fell by 12 per cent, from 43 deaths per 1,000 live births to 38. Additionally, the global neonatal mortality rate fell by about 10 per cent, from 20 deaths per 1,000 live births to 18. Despite this progress, 5 million children still lost their lives before their fifth birthday in 2021, down from 6.1 million in 2015. Nearly half of those deaths (2.3 million) occured in the first 28 days of life. While child mortality has declined in all regions, sub-Saharan Africa continues to face the highest rates. In 2021, 1 child in 14 died before reaching age 5 (74 deaths per 1,000 live births) in this region, the same as the global average rate achieved two decades ago in 2001.

By 2021, 133 countries had already met the SDG target on under-5 mortality, and an additional 13 are expected to do so by 2030, if current trends continue. But to achieve the target by 2030, progress needs to accelerate in 54 countries, nearly 75 per cent of which are in sub-Saharan Africa. If these countries were to achieve the under-5 target, nearly 10 million under-5 deaths could be averted between 2022 and 2030. Meanwhile, more than 60 countries need to accelerate progress to meet the neonatal target.

Under-5 and neonatal mortality rate, 2015–2021 (deaths per 1,000 live births)

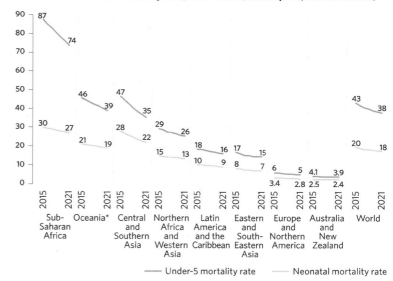

* Excluding Australia and New Zealand.

The alarming decline in childhood vaccination is leaving millions of children at risk from devastating but preventable diseases

The share of children who received three doses of the vaccine against diphtheria, tetanus and pertussis (DTP3) – a marker for immunization coverage within and across countries – fell 5 percentage points between 2019 and 2021, to just 81 per cent. This marked the largest sustained decline in childhood vaccinations in approximately 30 years. As a result, 25 million children missed out on one or more doses of DTP through routine immunization services in 2021 alone. This is 2 million more than those who missed out in 2020 and 6 million more than in 2019, highlighting the growing number of children at risk from devastating but preventable diseases. In 2021, only 70 per cent of children received two doses of the vaccine for measles, a highly contagious disease. This was far below the 95 per cent population coverage required to prevent outbreaks. Coverage of the first dose of human papillomavirus (HPV) vaccine, which has grave consequences for women and girls' health worldwide, reached only 15 per cent in 2021, despite the first vaccines being licensed over 15 years ago.

Measles-containing vaccination (MCV) coverage, 2015–2021 (percentage) and estimated number of children missing doses of MCV, 2015–2021 (millions)

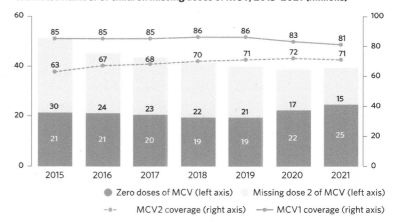

Intersecting crises have left the world off-kilter to achieve SDG targets on HIV, malaria and tuberculosis

HIV/AIDS: There were an estimated 1.5 million new human immunodeficiency virus (HIV) infections globally in 2021, almost one third fewer than in 2010. Effective HIV treatment has also cut global AIDS-related deaths by 52 per cent, from 1.4 million in 2010 to 650,000 in 2021. Sub-Saharan Africa, the region with the largest HIV burden, has achieved a 44 per cent decline in annual new HIV infections since 2010. However, the decline has been much sharper among males than among females. Fewer children were accessing treatment than adults. The aforementioned inequalities and others faced by key populations at increased risk of HIV are slowing progress towards ending AIDS. Moreover, new infections are rising in some regions, and the world is off track to meet the targets of fewer than 370,000 new HIV infections by 2025.

Tuberculosis (TB): The COVID-19 pandemic has severely impacted access to tuberculosis diagnosis and treatment in many countries, resulting in an increase in the TB disease burden globally. In 2021, an estimated 10.6 million people fell ill with TB, an increase from 10.1 million in 2020. The TB incidence rate also rose by 3.6 per cent between 2020 and 2021, reversing the decline of 2 per cent per year observed for most of the previous two decades. There were an estimated 1.6 million deaths from TB in 2021, an increase of 14.1 per cent from 2020. This is the first time in nearly two decades that the number of TB deaths has increased. Between 2015 and 2021, the net reductions in TB incidence and death were 10 per cent and 5.9 per cent, respectively, only one-fifth and one-tenth of the way to the 2025 milestone of WHO's End TB Strategy.

Malaria: In 2021, the global malaria death toll was estimated at 619,000, compared with 625,000 in 2020 and 568,000 in 2019. The total number of malaria cases worldwide reached 247 million in 2021, surpassing the figures of 245 million in 2020 and 232 million in 2019. Despite COVID-related disruptions, malaria-affected countries around the world largely maintained prevention, diagnosis and treatment measures at levels comparable to pre-pandemic times. In 2021, 128 million insecticide-treated nets reached their target destination, along with 223 million malaria rapid diagnostic tests and 242 million courses of artemisinin-based combination therapy. However, too many people at high risk of malaria are still missing out on the services they need to prevent, detect and treat the disease, and progress towards the ending malaria target by 2030 remains off course. In addition to pandemic-related disruptions, converging humanitarian crises, funding constraints, weak surveillance systems and declines in the effectiveness of core malaria-fighting tools threaten to undermine the global malaria response, particularly in Africa.

Neglected tropical diseases (NTDs): In 2021, 1.65 billion people were reported to require mass or individual treatment and care for neglected tropical diseases, down from 2.19 billion in 2010, representing a reduction of 25 per cent. As of December 2022, 47 countries, territories and areas have eliminated at least one NTD. In the LDCs, 46 per cent of the population required treatment and care for NTDs in 2021, down from 79 per cent in 2010.

HIV incidence rates, 2010 and 2021 (new cases per 1,000 uninfected adults aged 15–49 years)

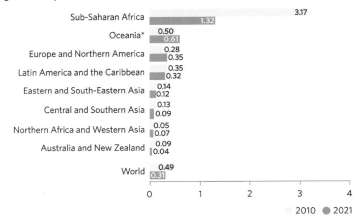

* Excluding Australia and New Zealand.

Incidence rate of tuberculosis, 2015–2021 (new cases per 100,000 population)

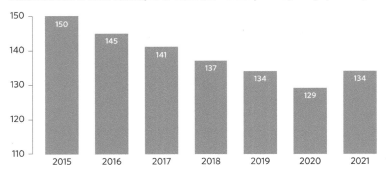

Two scenarios of global progress in the malaria incidence rate: current trajectory maintained and WHO Global Technical Strategy targets achieved, 2015–2030 (new cases per 100,000 population)

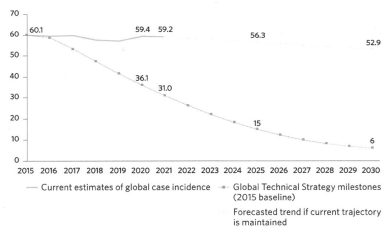

In the wake of the pandemic, progress towards universal health coverage has slowed while financial hardship has risen

Universal health coverage (UHC) aims to ensure that everyone can access quality health services without facing financial hardship. While efforts to combat infectious diseases like HIV, TB and malaria led to significant expansions in service coverage between 2000 and 2015, progress has since slowed. The UHC Service Coverage Index only increased by three points since 2015, reaching a score of 68 in 2021. Meanwhile, components of UHC related to non-communicable diseases, health service capacity and access have seen minimal or no progress.

Financial hardship remains a significant challenge. The proportion of the population spending over 10 per cent of their household budget on health, out of pocket, worsened from 12.6 per cent in 2015 to 13.5 per cent in 2019, affecting around 1 billion people. Additionally, 4.9 per cent of the global population (around 381 million people) were pushed or further pushed into extreme poverty due to out-of-pocket payments for health in 2019.

Available evidence suggests a pandemic-related deterioration in UHC, with subregional and country-level decreases in the Service Coverage Index and disruptions in the delivery of essential health services. COVID-19 has also led to higher rates of foregone care and increased financial hardship due to high and impoverishing out-of-pocket spending. Accelerating the expansion of essential health services, particularly in areas with minimal progress, is crucial for advancing UHC. Proactive policies are needed to reduce financial hardship, increase public health funding, extend coverage for medicines and remove co-payments for the poor.

Despite increases in the global health workforce, numbers remain low in regions with the highest burden of disease

A 2020 study shows that the projected global shortage of health workers by 2030 has been reduced from 18 million to 10 million. Despite a significant increase in the overall size of the global health workforce, regions with the highest disease burden continue to have the lowest proportion of health workers to deliver health services. Between 2014 and 2021, sub-Saharan Africa continues to have the lowest health worker density, with only 2.3 medical doctors and 12.6 nursing and midwifery personnel per 10,000 population. In contrast, Europe had the highest density for doctors, at 39.4 per 10,000 population, while Northern America had the most nursing and midwifery personnel, with 152.1 per 10,000 population. Even when national densities seem adequate, disparities persist between rural, remote, subnational and hard-to-reach areas compared with capital cities and urban centres.

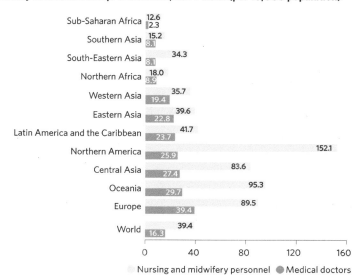

Density of select health professionals, 2014–2021 (per 10,000 population)

Region	Nursing and midwifery personnel	Medical doctors
Sub-Saharan Africa	12.6	2.3
Southern Asia	15.2	8.1
South-Eastern Asia	34.3	8.1
Northern Africa	18.0	8.9
Western Asia	35.7	19.4
Eastern Asia	39.6	22.8
Latin America and the Caribbean	41.7	23.7
Northern America	152.1	25.9
Central Asia	83.6	27.4
Oceania	95.3	29.7
Europe	89.5	39.4
World	39.4	16.3

Driven by COVID-19, official development assistance for basic health has doubled since 2015

Official development assistant (ODA) for basic health from all donors has doubled in real terms since 2015, from $10.2 billion (constant 2021 prices) to $20.4 billion in 2021. Approximately $2.7 billion was spent on basic health care, $2.4 billion on malaria control, and $2.0 billion on infectious disease control. Germany, the United States, the Global Fund and Gavi, the Vaccine Alliance, accounted for almost 40 per cent of this total. In 2021, COVID-19 control represented the largest share of ODA for basic health, totaling $9.6 billion, of which $6.3 billion was for vaccine donations. Preliminary data for 2022 indicate that within total ODA, $11.2 billion was spent on COVID-19-related activities,[2] down 45 per cent from 2021. Vaccine donations amounted to $1.53 billion, a fall of 74 per cent in real terms compared to 2021.

---

2   The figures in 2022 on COVID-19-related activities are preliminary and partial, as several donors are still in the process of collecting detailed information, especially sector-related data.

Quality education

Maria, 9, learns from pre-recorded lessons on her father's phone at the Kili internally displaced persons camp in Syria. A distance-learning platform was designed to ensure education for displaced and refugee children.

- Progress towards quality education was already slower than required before the pandemic, but COVID-19 has had devastating impacts on education, causing learning losses in four out of five of the 104 countries studied.

- Without additional measures, only one in six countries will achieve the universal secondary school completion target by 2030, an estimated 84 million children and young people will still be out of school, and approximately 300 million students will lack the basic numeracy and literacy skills necessary for success in life.

- To achieve national Goal 4 benchmarks, which are reduced in ambition compared with the original Goal 4 targets, 79 low- and lower-middle-income countries still face an average annual financing gap of $97 billion.

- To deliver on Goal 4, education financing must become a national investment priority. Furthermore, measures such as making education free and compulsory, increasing the number of teachers, improving basic school infrastructure and embracing digital transformation are essential.

Primary and secondary school completion is rising, but the pace is far too slow and uneven

Between 2015 and 2021, worldwide primary school completion increased from 85 to 87 per cent, lower secondary completion rose from 74 to 77 per cent and upper secondary completion grew from 53 to 58 per cent. However, the pace of improvement was significantly slower than the 2000–2015 period. Most regions have primary completion rates of nearly 90 per cent or higher, except sub-Saharan Africa, where fewer than two-thirds of children complete primary school. In impoverished regions, poor learning outcomes lead to high drop-out rates and delayed completion. In sub-Saharan Africa, although 80 per cent of primary-aged children are enrolled in school, only 62 per cent graduate on time. Economic burdens, like expenses for books and uniforms, plus opportunity costs, also contribute to incomplete education.

Since 2019, UNESCO Member States have participated in a national Goal 4 benchmarking process to set national education targets. Despite the aspiration of universal secondary school completion, only one in six countries aims to achieve this goal by 2030 based on their national targets. Even if these targets are met, an estimated 84 million children and young people will still be out of school by 2030.

School completion rate, by level of education, 2015 and 2021 (percentage)

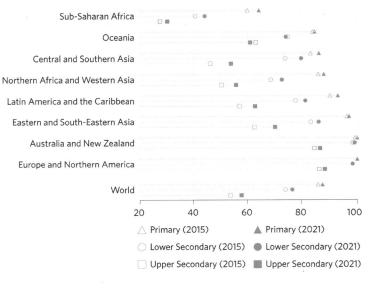

Patchy data show disappointing progress on improving primary school reading levels

In 2015, approximately 60 per cent of students demonstrated minimum proficiency in reading across primary and lower secondary schools. However, achieving universal minimum learning proficiency by 2030 requires an average annual improvement of around 2.7 percentage points. Despite positive gains between 2000 and 2019, progress was minimal and significantly slower than required. Examining reading levels at the end of primary school, trend data covering 34 per cent of the world's children reveal an annual improvement of 0.39 percentage points, less than one seventh of what's needed. However, comprehensive trend data to fully assess progress are lacking. Enhancing national and cross-national assessments is crucial for effective monitoring.

The pandemic has had devastating impacts on learning. Learning losses due to COVID-related school closures were documented in four in five of the 104 countries studied. A recent Progress in International Reading Literacy Study assessment revealed declines in 21 out of 32 countries with comparable data from 2016–2021, and parents reported also that two thirds of students experienced learning setbacks due to prolonged periods at home. Another study in seven high-income countries found COVID-19-related learning losses equivalent to 30 per cent of a school year for mathematics and 35 per cent for reading if schools were closed for eight weeks. According to national education targets, the percentage of students attaining basic reading skills by the end of primary school is projected to rise from 51 per cent in 2015 to 67 per cent by 2030. However, an estimated 300 million children and young people will still lack basic numeracy and literacy skills by 2030.

Access to early childhood education has expanded, but progress has slowed since 2015

Early schooling stimulates children's readiness for school and improves their future learning experience. In 2020, three out of four children globally were enrolled in organized learning one year before the official primary entry age, with progress stagnating since 2015. The pandemic caused temporary dips in pre-primary education participation, with 30 out of 52 countries with data for 2021 or after witnessing declines. Only half of children were enrolled in organized learning one year before the official primary entry age in sub-Saharan Africa and in Northern Africa and Western Asia in 2020. The average attendance rate of early childhood education for children aged 36–59 months in 61 low- and middle-income countries was 37 per cent, with a 16-percentage-point gap between urban and rural areas and a 34-percentage-point gap between the richest and poorest quintiles. As of 2020, only half of the 187 countries and areas with data provided free pre-primary education, and almost three quarters of the 215 countries and areas with data did not make pre-primary education compulsory. Failure to eliminate school fees risks entrenching inequality. About 40 per cent of countries have not achieved gender parity.

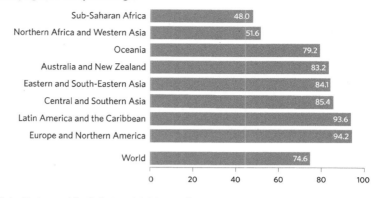

Participation rate in organized learning (one year before the official primary entry age), 2020 (percentage)

Sub-Saharan Africa	48.0
Northern Africa and Western Asia	51.6
Oceania	79.2
Australia and New Zealand	83.2
Eastern and South-Eastern Asia	84.1
Central and Southern Asia	85.4
Latin America and the Caribbean	93.6
Europe and Northern America	94.2
World	74.6

Note: "Eastern and South-Eastern Asia" data are from 2019.

Low digital skills hamper progress towards universal and meaningful connectivity

Low levels of information and communications technology (ICT) skills are a major barrier to achieving universal and meaningful connectivity. Data on digital skills are limited, only available in 78 countries and rarely for all five categories of skills (communication/collaboration; problem-solving; safety; content creation; and information/data literacy). While 86 per cent of individuals use the Internet in countries providing data, many lack the required digital skills to be able to fully benefit from it or avoid its dangers. Communication/collaboration skills are the most prevalent, followed by problem-solving, safety and content creation. Information/data literacy varies widely between countries. Among 74 countries that provided data on at least three skills areas, only five reported averages of over 75 per cent in multiple areas.

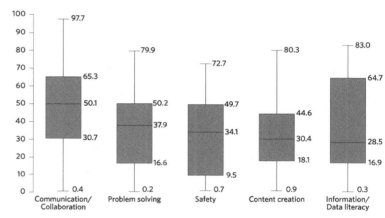

Proportion of youth and adults with ICT skills, by type of skill, 2019–2021

Note: The bars indicate the 25th, median and 75th percentile of all country values. The bottom and top lines indicate the minimum and maximum values (excluding outliers).

Basic school infrastructure varies widely across regions and is far from universal

Access to basic school facilities is essential for safe and conducive learning environments, but one in four primary schools globally lacks basic services like electricity, water, sanitation and handwashing facilities. Access to computers, the Internet and disability-adapted facilities is even lower, with fewer than one in two primary schools having access, on average. Access is higher in lower and upper secondary schools. Regions with the lowest access to basic facilities include Central and Southern Asia, sub-Saharan Africa, and Latin America and the Caribbean. However, some progress has been made, with primary school electricity access increasing by over 10 percentage points since 2012. Access to computers and disability-adapted facilities,

essential for marginalized students' participation, has also improved by almost 5 percentage points.

Adequate infrastructure is also important for mitigating COVID-19 transmission and ensuring safe education. In early 2021, fewer than 10 per cent of low-income countries reported having sufficient soap, clean water, masks, and sanitation and hygiene facilities to assure the safety of all learners and staff, compared with 96 per cent in high-income countries. Investment and monitoring of infrastructure should be a policy priority to prevent the further entrenchment of inequalities.

Many teachers still lack the required qualifications to teach

Ensuring that all teachers possess the minimum qualifications required for their profession is crucial for achieving quality education. However, in 2020, more than 14 per cent of teachers were still not qualified according to national norms, with considerable disparities between countries and across regions. Sub-Saharan Africa faces the biggest challenge, with the lowest

percentages of trained teachers in pre-primary (60 per cent), primary (69 per cent) and secondary education (61 per cent) among all regions. The COVID-19 pandemic severely disrupted education, affecting the teaching workforce in most countries. To maintain access, teachers had to adapt to new pedagogical concepts and methods, for which many were unprepared.

Gender equality

- With only seven years remaining, a mere 15.4 per cent of Goal 5 indicators with data are "on track", 61.5 per cent are at a moderate distance and 23.1 per cent are far or very far off track from 2030 targets.

- In many areas, progress has been too slow. At the current rate, it will take an estimated 300 years to end child marriage, 286 years to close gaps in legal protection and remove discriminatory laws, 140 years for women to be represented equally in positions of power and leadership in the workplace, and 47 years to achieve equal representation in national parliaments.

- Political leadership, investments and comprehensive policy reforms are needed to dismantle systemic barriers to achieving Goal 5. Gender equality is a cross-cutting objective and must be a key focus of national policies, budgets and institutions.

Women from different social organizations participate in a march against gender violence in Quito, Ecuador.

Progress has been sluggish on upping women's share in management and political representation

As of 1 January 2023, the global share of women in lower and single chambers of national parliaments reached 26.5 per cent – a slight improvement of 4.2 percentage points since 2015, but an average annual increase of just 0.5 points. At the local level, women held 35.5 per cent of seats in local governments in 2023, up from 33.9 per cent in 2020. If current trends continue, it will take more than four decades to close the gender gap in national parliamentary representation and three decades to do so at the local level. Legislated gender quotas have proven effective, with countries applying quotas seeing an average of 30.9 per cent women's representation in the 2022 parliamentary elections, compared with 21.2 per cent in countries without quotas. Quotas also contribute to higher women's representation in local government, by seven percentage points on average.

Globally, women accounted for nearly 40 per cent of total employment but held only 28.2 per cent of management positions in 2021. Progress on increasing women's representation in management has been slow, with only a 1.0-percentage-point increase since 2015. At the current rate, it would take more than 140 years to achieve gender parity in managerial positions. Women's representation in management remains below their share in total employment across all regions, with sub-Saharan Africa making the most progress, reaching 38.2 per cent in 2021. Conversely, Northern Africa and

Western Asia, and Central and Southern Asia, have the lowest shares of women in management positions, at around 15 per cent, linked to low female employment rates in those regions.

Proportion of seats held by women in national parliaments and local governments (percentage)

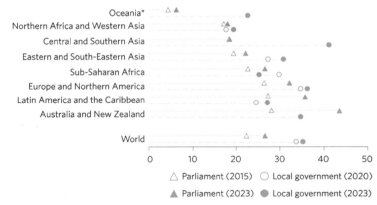

△ Parliament (2015)   ○ Local government (2020)
▲ Parliament (2023)   ● Local government (2023)

*Excluding Australia and New Zealand.

Nearly half of married women lack decision-making power over their sexual and reproductive health and rights

Only 56 per cent of women aged 15 to 49 who are married or in a union are able to make decisions about their sexual and reproductive health and rights, according to data collected from 68 countries for the 2007–2022 period. Disparities exist among regions, ranging from 37 per cent in sub-Saharan Africa to over 80 per cent in some countries in Europe and Latin America and the Caribbean. While 89 per cent of women can decide to use contraception, one in four lack the autonomy to make health care decisions or to refuse sex.

Around 76 per cent of the 115 countries analysed have supportive laws and regulations guaranteeing full and equal access to sexual and reproductive health and rights. Barriers to accessing sexual and reproductive health care, information and education persist due to the lack of positive laws or the presence of negative ones, particularly in relation to abortion, the human papillomavirus (HPV) vaccine and sex education. Key components for ensuring sexual and reproductive health and rights laws include budget allocations, technical guidance, health worker training and public awareness-raising.

Insufficient progress has been made in reducing intimate partner violence over the past two decades

Despite growing global awareness and evidence on effective prevention strategies, progress on reducing violence against women and girls over the past two decades has been inadequate. Globally, in 2000, 35 per cent of ever-partnered women aged 15–49 had been subjected to physical and/or sexual violence by a male partner or ex-partner in their lifetimes and 16 per cent were subjected to this form of violence within the past 12 months. By 2018, these figures had dropped to 31 per cent of women for lifetime prevalence and 13 per cent for past-year prevalence. However, existing evidence suggests that violence against women was exacerbated by the pandemic. Without dedicated investment in scaling up prevention programmes, implementing effective policies and providing support services to address violence, countries will not achieve the target of eliminating violence against women and girls by 2030.

Discriminatory laws and gaps in legal protection persist in critical aspects, denying women their human rights worldwide

Data collected in 2022 from 119 countries reveal ongoing challenges for women in accessing their full human rights due to discriminatory laws and gaps in legal protection. An astonishing 55 per cent of countries lack laws that explicitly prohibit direct and indirect discrimination against women; 60 per cent lack laws that define rape based on the principle of consent. Another 45 per cent do not mandate equal remuneration for work of equal value, while more than a third of countries fail to provide maternity leave in accordance with International Labour Organization (ILO) standards. In terms of marriage and family, nearly a quarter of countries do not grant equal rights in marriage and divorce and close to three-quarters fail to establish 18 years as the minimum age of marriage for both women and men, without exceptions. Closing gaps in legal protections and removing discriminatory laws could take up to 286 years based on the current rate of change.

Recent gains are under threat in efforts to end child marriage

Today one in five young women (19 per cent) were married before their 18th birthday, compared with one in four (25 per cent) 25 years ago. Notable progress has been made in countries like Bangladesh, Ethiopia, India, Maldives and Rwanda. However, there has been little progress in areas of sub-Saharan Africa where child marriage is highest, and levels have remained stagnant in Latin America and the Caribbean. Furthermore, girls from the richest households are still much more likely to see progress than girls from the poorest households.

At the current pace, the world is at least 300 years away from ending child marriage and more than 9 million girls will still be married in the year 2030. Additional challenges related to the COVID-19 pandemic, conflicts and the impacts of climate change threaten to further hamper progress. Pandemic impacts alone are expected to result in an additional 10 million girls becoming child brides by 2030.

Projected number of girls under age 18 married per year, 2023–2030 projections (millions)

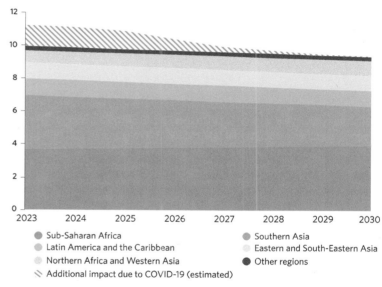

Note: "Other regions" include Europe and Northern America, Central Asia and Oceania.

Agricultural land ownership and legal protection of women's land rights remain low

Available data from 46 countries for 2009–2020 show that many women and men involved in agricultural production lack ownership and/or secure tenure rights over agricultural land. In one third of these countries, less than 50 per cent of women and men have land ownership or secure rights. Meanwhile, in almost half of these countries, the share of men with ownership is at least twice that of women. When it comes to legal frameworks, close to 60 per cent of the 71 reporting countries have no or low levels of protection for women's land rights. However, positive examples of laws and policies promoting women's land rights exist in all regions, particularly in marital property and inheritance. Moreover, 51 per cent of the 41 countries with laws recognizing customary law or customary land tenure explicitly protect women's land rights. Many also provide mandatory quotas to ensure women's representation in land management and administration institutions. Nonetheless, there is a need for stronger protection, policies and enforcement of laws to safeguard women's land rights.

Mobile phone ownership can be a powerful tool for empowering women, but gender parity remains elusive in many regions

Owning a mobile phone has been shown to be an important tool to empower women by connecting them to other people and enabling them to access information and services. Globally, 73 per cent of the population aged 10 and over owned a mobile phone in 2022, up from 67 per cent in 2019. However, women were 12 per cent less likely to own mobile phones than men, a gap that has remained relatively unchanged since 2019. Significant disparities exist across regions, with gender parity largely reached or almost reached in high- and middle-income regions, but far from achieved in lower-income regions. The gender gaps are twice as high (reaching around 25 per cent) in Central and Southern Asia and sub-Saharan Africa.

6 CLEAN WATER AND SANITATION

Clean water and sanitation

- Despite great progress, billions of people still lack access to safe drinking water, sanitation and hygiene. Achieving universal coverage by 2030 will require a substantial increase in current global rates of progress: sixfold for drinking water, fivefold for sanitation and threefold for hygiene.

- Water use efficiency has risen by 9 per cent, but water stress and water scarcity remain a concern in many parts of the world. In 2020, 2.4 billion people lived in water-stressed countries. The challenges are compounded by conflicts and climate change.

- Key strategies to get Goal 6 back on track include increasing sector-wide investment and capacity-building, promoting innovation and evidence-based action, enhancing cross-sectoral coordination and cooperation among all stakeholders, and adopting a more integrated and holistic approach to water management.

Fatuma pours water, obtained from a recently installed solar-powered borehole, for her family's baby goats in drought-stricken Somalia.

Access to drinking water, sanitation and hygiene improved significantly in rural areas, but stagnated or decreased in urban areas

Between 2015 and 2022, the proportion of the world's population with access to safely managed drinking water services increased from 69 to 73 per cent; safely managed sanitation services increased from 49 to 57 per cent; and basic hygiene services increased from 67 to 75 per cent. This progress signifies an additional 687 million, 911 million and 637 million people gaining access to these essential services, respectively. Open defecation decreased from 715 million to 419 million during this period. However, in 2022, 2.2 billion people still lacked safely managed drinking water, including 703 million without a basic water service; 3.5 billion people lacked safely managed sanitation, including 1.5 billion without basic sanitation services; and 2 billion lacked a basic handwashing facility with soap and water at home, including 653 million with no handwashing facility at all. Sub-Saharan Africa is furthest behind. During this period, while the rural population saw improvements in access, the urban population's access remained largely unchanged or decreased. To achieve universal coverage by 2030, the current rates of progress would need to increase by three to six times.

Global urban and rural population without safely managed drinking water, safely managed sanitation, and basic hygiene services, 2015/17–2022 (billions)

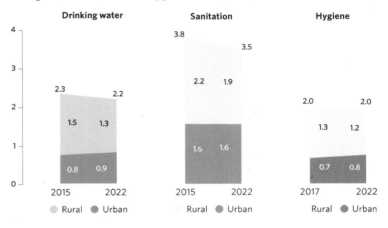

Water quality is improving in countries with robust monitoring, but there are still many unknowns

Progress towards the target of halving the proportion of untreated wastewater by 2030 is limited. Based on data from 140 countries and territories, about 58 per cent of household wastewater was safely treated in 2022. However, wastewater statistics are lacking in many countries and reporting is low, especially from industrial sources.

Data from 2017–2020 indicate that 60 per cent of assessed water bodies in 97 countries had good ambient water quality. Countries with robust monitoring systems showed positive trends: 44 per cent of countries reporting in both 2017 and 2020 were on track to improve water quality. However, a lack of data poses a risk to more than 3 billion people living in areas where the quality of freshwater is unknown. Agriculture and untreated wastewater are major threats to water quality, with nitrogen and phosphorus measurements frequently failing to meet targets. Efforts are needed to improve farming practices and wastewater treatment, especially in regions with high population growth.

Proportion of bodies of water with good ambient water quality, 2017–2020 (percentage)

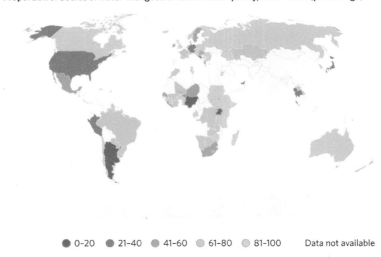

● 0–20 ● 21–40 ● 41–60 ● 61–80 ○ 81–100 Data not available

Water-use efficiency has improved, particularly in agriculture, but rising water stress in several areas is cause for concern

Although global water stress levels (the ratio of freshwater withdrawn to total renewable freshwater resources) remained at a safe level of 18.2 per cent in 2020, this masks substantial regional variations. Central and Southern Asia experience high water stress levels, exceeding 75 per cent, and Northern Africa faces critical water stress, surpassing 100 per cent. The region of Northern Africa and Western Asia has seen a concerning 18 per cent increase in water stress between 2015 and 2020. An estimated 2.4 billion people lived in water-stressed countries in 2020, of which almost 800 million lived in high and critically high water-stressed countries.

Improving water-use efficiency is one key to reducing water stress. Water-use efficiency worldwide rose 9 per cent, from $17.4/m3 in 2015 to $18.9/m³ in 2020. It ranges from below $3/m³ in economies that depend on agriculture to over $50/m³ in highly industrialized or service-based economies. The agriculture sector experienced the greatest increase in water-use efficiency (20 per cent) from 2015, compared with the industrial and service sectors (13 and 0.3 per cent, respectively). Improving water-use efficiency will require more efficient irrigation, better agricultural management, tackling leakages in distribution networks and optimizing industrial and energy cooling processes.

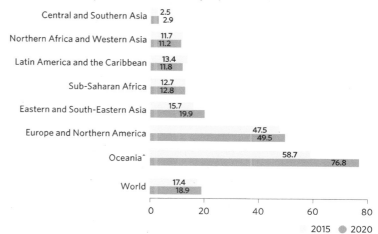

Water-use efficiency, 2015 and 2020 (USD/m³)

Region	2015	2020
Central and Southern Asia	2.5	2.9
Northern Africa and Western Asia	11.7	11.2
Latin America and the Caribbean	13.4	11.8
Sub-Saharan Africa	12.7	12.8
Eastern and South-Eastern Asia	15.7	19.9
Europe and Northern America	47.5	49.5
Oceania^	58.7	76.8
World	17.4	18.9

Note: Oceania^ includes only data from Australia, New Zealand and Fiji.

Enhancing water management and transboundary cooperation is critical for bolstering resilience to crises

A lack of both cross-sector coordination over water and operational arrangements for transboundary water cooperation threatens the achievement of targets on climate, food, energy, health, life on land and below water, and peace. Although there has been global progress on integrated water resources management between 2017 and 2020, with the overall score increasing from 49 to 54 out of 100, it falls far short of meeting target 6.5 of implementing integrated water resources management at all levels by 2030. Encouragingly, 44 countries have nearly achieved the target and 22 countries have proved that real and rapid progress is possible, but urgent acceleration is needed in 107 countries. Out of 153 countries sharing transboundary rivers, lakes and aquifers, only 32 have 90 per cent or more of their transboundary waters covered by operational arrangements, suggesting that significant efforts are needed to ensure that all shared rivers, lakes and aquifers are covered by 2030. The world must accelerate all aspects of water management, together with transboundary cooperation, to increase its resilience to crises – including climate, health and poverty.

Integrated water-resources-management implementation progress, 2017–2020

○ Limited (55)   ◐ Moderate (52)   ◕ Substantial (22)
● Close to target (44)   ○ No trend

Note: Number of countries progress per level in parentheses.

Decline in official development assistance to water sector raises concerns

Official development assistance (ODA) disbursements to the water sector decreased by 15 per cent between 2015 and 2021, from $9.6 billion to $8.1 billion. Total ODA commitments to the water sector have also fallen 12 per cent, from $11.2 billion in 2015 to $9.8 billion in 2021. Commitments peaked at $13.5 billion in 2017 and have decreased every year since. Sub-Saharan Africa received the largest share – 28 per cent or more of water-sector ODA disbursements every year since 2015 – but all SDG regions saw decreased disbursements from 2019 to 2021. Additionally, donor alignment with national water-sector plans remains low, with only 29 per cent of countries reporting high alignment in 2021.

As wetland ecosystems and species disappear, large-scale protection and restoration are imperative

Water-related ecosystems provide clean water, regulate floods and droughts and support biodiversity. But these ecosystems face numerous threats, including pollution, climate change and overexploitation. The extent of surface water bodies, such as lakes, rivers and reservoirs, are rapidly changing worldwide, with one in five river basins experiencing above-natural fluctuations in surface water over the past five years. Wetland ecosystems have suffered an alarming 85 per cent loss in the past three centuries, primarily from drainage and land conversion. Since 1970, a staggering 81 per cent of species dependent on inland wetlands have declined, surpassing declines in other biomes, and an increasing number are at risk of extinction. It is imperative to prioritize the protection and restoration of wetlands on a large scale.

Affordable and clean energy

- The world continues to advance towards sustainable energy targets – but not fast enough. At the current pace, about 660 million people will still lack access to electricity and close to 2 billion people will still rely on polluting fuels and technologies for cooking by 2030.

- Renewable sources power nearly 30 per cent of energy consumption in the electricity sector, but challenges remain in heating and transport sectors. Developing countries experience 9.6 per cent annual growth in renewable energy installation, but despite enormous needs, international financial flows for clean energy continue to decline.

- To ensure access to energy for all by 2030, we must accelerate electrification, increase investments in renewable energy, improve energy efficiency and develop enabling policies and regulatory frameworks.

In Lebanon, women install solar panels as part of efforts to empower women in the renewable energy sector, improving their skills for economic empowerment during crises and the pandemic.

More people than ever have access to electricity, but the pace is lagging for least developed countries

The global electricity access rate increased from 87 per cent in 2015 to 91 per cent in 2021, serving close to an additional 800 million people. However, 675 million people still lacked access to electricity in 2021, mostly located in LDCs. Despite steady progress in the last six years, the annual access growth rate of 0.6 percentage points between 2019 and 2021 lags behind the 0.8 percentage points observed in 2015–2019. In sub-Saharan Africa, due to population growth, the number of people without access has remained stubbornly stagnant since 2010, leaving 567 million without access in 2021. Electrification can help increase educational attainment, improve health care, support agriculture development, reduce gender inequality, enhance climate action and create business opportunities and jobs. However, if the current pace continues, some 660 million people will still be without electricity by 2030. To change course and achieve universal access by 2030, the access rate must increase by 1 percentage point annually between 2021 and 2030.

Proportion of population with access to electricity, 2015 and 2021 (percentage)

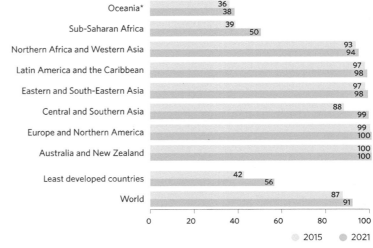

* Excluding Australia and New Zealand.

At the current pace, a quarter of the population will still be using unsafe and inefficient cooking systems by 2030

In 2021, around 2.3 billion people – 29 per cent of the global population – were still relying on inefficient and polluting cooking systems, jeopardizing their health, limiting their life opportunities, and damaging the climate and environment. Between 2015 and 2021, the proportion of people with access to clean cooking fuels and technologies increased only by 7 percentage points. However, South-Eastern Asia saw significant and consistent progress, achieving access for around three-quarters of its population in 2021, up 14 percentage points from 2015. Conversely, the region with the lowest access rates was sub-Saharan Africa, where progress towards clean cooking has failed to keep pace with growing populations, leaving a total of 0.9 billion people without access in 2021. If current trends continue, only 77 per cent of the global population will have access to clean cooking solutions by 2030, leaving nearly 1.9 billion people behind, including 1.1 billion in sub-Saharan Africa.

Absolute number of people and proportion of the global population with access to clean cooking fuels and technologies, 2015–2021 (billions and percentage)

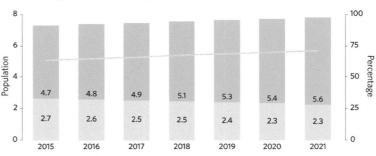

- Population with access to clean fuels and technologies for cooking (left axis)
- Population without access to clean fuels and technologies for cooking (left axis)
- Percentage of the global population with access to clean cooking fuels and technologies (right axis)

Renewable energy use is growing in the electricity sector, but limited in heating and transport

Globally, in 2020, renewable sources accounted for 19.1 per cent of total final energy consumption, representing a 2.4-percentage-point increase from 2015. Over the same period, total renewable energy consumption increased by 16 per cent. Traditional uses of biomass – such as the burning of wood in open stoves or fireplaces – still represented over a third of total renewable energy use in 2020. But modern renewable sources are slowly expanding, from 10 per cent of total final energy consumption in 2015 to 12.5 per cent in 2020. The electricity sector shows the largest share of renewables in total final energy consumption (28.2 per cent in 2020). However, progress in the heating and transport sectors has been limited over the past decade, as upward trends in demand have outpaced the deployment of renewables. Meeting the targets of Goal 7 and the Paris Agreement will require sustained policy momentum to scale up both renewable energy deployment and energy conservation in all sectors, as well as to mobilize public and private investment, particularly in developing countries.

Share of renewable sources in final energy consumption and by end use, 2015 and 2020 (percentage)

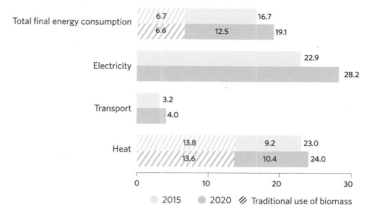

A strong rebound is needed to reach energy efficiency targets

Global primary energy intensity, defined as the ratio of total energy supply to GDP – in essence, the amount of energy used per unit of wealth created – improved from 4.96 megajoules per dollar (2017 purchasing power parity) in 2015 to 4.63 in 2020, representing an average annual improvement rate of 1.4 per cent. This is well below the 2.6 per cent required to meet target 7.3 of doubling the global rate of improvement in energy efficiency by 2030 (compared with the baseline rate of 1990–2010). In 2020, the improvement rate slowed down to 0.6 per cent, due to the COVID-19 crisis, marking the smallest gains since the global financial crisis. It is expected that energy intensity will improve at a higher pace in 2022. However, to make up for lost time, energy intensity improvements will need to average 3.4 per cent per year until 2030. Prioritizing energy efficiency in policy and increasing investment can help the world achieve energy and climate targets.

Annual change of global primary energy intensity, 1990–2020 (percentage)

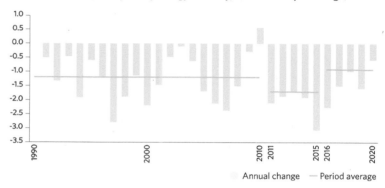

International public financing for clean energy in developing countries continues to decline

International public financial flows in support of clean energy in developing countries have been on a decreasing trend, starting even before the COVID-19 pandemic and continuing through 2021. They amounted to $10.8 billion in 2021, down by nearly 12 per cent from 2020. This was 35 per cent less than the 2010–2019 decade-long average, and less than half the 2017 peak of $26.4 billion. In 2021, the distribution of financial flows by technology shifted from hydropower to solar energy: with solar accounting for 43 per cent; other renewables garnering 33 per cent of flows; and the lowest number of commitments being for hydropower (16 per cent), and wind and geothermal energy (8 per cent combined). These decreasing trends jeopardize the chances of achieving energy goals, particularly for LDCs, landlocked developing countries (LLDCs) and small island developing States (SIDS).

Renewable energy is booming in developing countries, but the least developed are falling behind

In 2021, developing countries installed a record-breaking 268 watts per capita of renewable energy-generating capacity, following two decades of steady increases that have consistently outpaced population growth. The compound annual growth rate of renewable energy in developing countries from 2016–2021 was 9.6 per cent, compared to 8.6 per cent for 2010–2015. But despite this positive and accelerating growth, developing countries are still not on track to meet SDG 7.b targets by 2030, and those countries most in need are being left behind. From 2016 to 2021, the annual growth rate was significantly lower for SIDS (8.5 per cent), LDCs (5.5 per cent) and LLDCs (3.8 per cent). At current rates, LDCs would need almost 40 years, LLDCs 25 and SIDS 13 years to reach the same level of deployment that developing countries overall achieved in 2021. Closing these gaps will require tailored policies and investments to ensure a just and climate-safe energy transition.

Decent work and economic growth

Anisa, who turned to the profession of electronic device repairs to help women customers, mends a laptop at her phone and computer maintenance shop in Yemen.

- Multiple crises are placing the global economy under serious threat. Global real GDP per capita growth is forecast to slow down in 2023. Challenging economic conditions are pushing more workers into informal employment.

- As economies start to recover, the global unemployment rate has experienced a significant decline. However, the youth unemployment rate continues to be much higher than the rate for adults, indicating ongoing challenges in securing employment opportunities for young people.

- The pandemic has accelerated digital adoption and transformed access to finance. Globally, 76 per cent of adults had bank accounts or accounts with regulated institutions in 2021, up from 62 per cent in 2014.

- Achieving Goal 8 will require a wholesale reform of the financial system to tackle rising debts, economic uncertainty and trade tensions, while promoting equitable pay and decent work for young people.

Global economic recovery continues on a slow trajectory

The global economy is grappling with persistent inflation, increasing interest rates and heightened uncertainties. Global real GDP per capita increased at an average annual rate of 1.8 per cent from 2015 to 2019, then sharply declined by 4.1 per cent in 2020 due to the COVID-19 pandemic. It then rebounded in 2021 with a solid 5.2 per cent increase, only to decelerate to 2.2 per cent in 2022. Estimates are that growth will further dwindle, to 1.4 per cent in 2023, followed by a modest increase of 1.6 per cent in 2024.

In LDCs, the annual growth rate of real GDP dropped from 5 per cent in 2019 to just 0.2 per cent in 2020 before recovering to 2.8 per cent in 2021. However, it is estimated that growth will resume, with the annual rate rising to 4.3 per cent in 2022 and further increasing by 4.1 per cent and 5.2 per cent in 2023 and 2024, respectively. However, these growth rates still fall short of the SDG target of 7 per cent.

Annual growth rate of global real GDP per capita and annual growth rate of real GDP of LDCs, 2015–2024 (percentage)

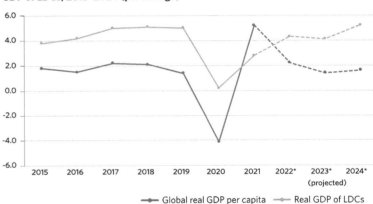

Challenging economic conditions are pushing more workers into informal employment

Before the pandemic, the incidence of informal employment had been slowly declining, from 58.6 per cent in 2015 to 57.8 per cent in 2019. However, COVID-19 lockdowns and containment measures resulted in disproportionate job losses for informal workers, particularly women. The subsequent recovery was driven by informal employment, which saw a slight uptick, reaching 58.0 per cent in 2022. This corresponds to around 2 billion workers in precarious jobs without social protection.

The situation was most alarming in LDCs, where informal employment stood at 89.7 per cent in 2022, with no improvement since 2015. Sub-Saharan Africa and Central and Southern Asia also continued to have high informality rates, at 87.2 per cent and 84.8 per cent, respectively. Women have been worse off during the employment recovery, with four out of five jobs created in 2022 for women being informal, compared to only two out of three jobs for men.

Proportion of informal employment, 2015-2022 (percentage)

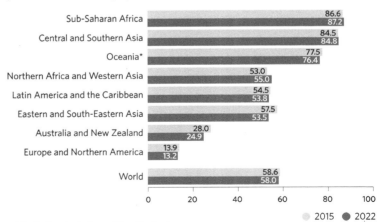

* Excluding Australia and New Zealand.

Global unemployment is expected to decline below pre-pandemic levels, but challenges persist in low-income countries

The global unemployment rate declined significantly in 2022, falling to 5.4 per cent from a peak of 6.6 per cent in 2020 as economies began recovering from the shock of the COVID-19 pandemic. This rate was lower than the pre-pandemic level of 5.5 per cent in 2019. The estimated total global unemployment in 2022 was 192 million. Projections indicate that global unemployment is expected to decrease further to 5.3 per cent in 2023, equivalent to 191 million people. This decline reflects greater-than-anticipated labour market resilience in high-income countries in the face of the economic slowdown. However, low-income countries are unlikely to see such declines in unemployment in 2023.

The pandemic disproportionately affected women and youth in labour markets. Women experienced a stronger recovery in employment and labour force participation than men. However, young people aged 15–24 continue to face severe difficulties in securing decent employment, and the global youth unemployment rate is much higher than the rate for adults aged 25 and above.

Unemployment rate, 2019, 2020, 2022 and 2023 projections (percentage)

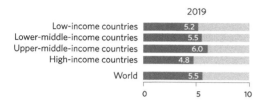
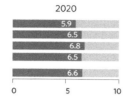
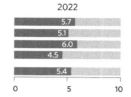

	2019	2020	2022	2023 projections
Low-income countries	5.2	5.9	5.7	5.7
Lower-middle-income countries	5.5	6.5	5.1	5.1
Upper-middle-income countries	6.0	6.8	6.0	5.7
High-income countries	4.8	6.5	4.5	4.6
World	5.5	6.6	5.4	5.3

Young women are more than twice as likely as young men to be out of education, employment or training

Globally, nearly 1 in 4 young people (23.5 per cent or 289 million) were not in education, employment or training (NEET) in 2022. While this is a slight decrease from the peak in 2020, it remains higher than pre-pandemic levels and also above the 2015 baseline of 22.2 per cent. Across regions, the situation remains most dire for young people in Central and Southern Asia and in Northern Africa and Western Asia, with NEET rates of 31.4 and 28.8 per cent, respectively. Meanwhile, sub-Saharan Africa recorded the highest rate increase from 2015 to 2022, with now more than a quarter of young people in the region not in education, employment or training.

Alarmingly, young women remained more than twice as likely (32.1 per cent) as young men (15.4 per cent) to not be in education, employment or training in 2022. Efforts to reduce youth NEET rates, especially among young women, need to be intensified to address the long-term impacts on their economic potential and future opportunities.

Share of youth not in education, employment or training by sex, 2022 (percentage)

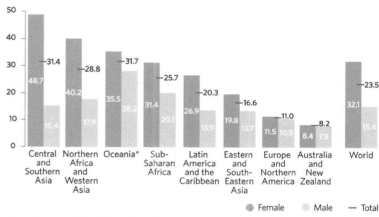

* Excluding Australia and New Zealand.

Tourism is on a path to recovery, but still well below pre-pandemic levels

Tourism has been severely impacted by the COVID-19 pandemic. In 2020, the share of tourism in global GDP was nearly halved by the pandemic. There was a modest 6 per cent improvement in 2021, with the sector's contribution to global GDP reaching 2.5 per cent. While this indicates that tourism is on a path to recovery, it is still considerably below the pre-pandemic level of 4.2 per cent in 2019. The recovery and economic contributions of the tourism industry varied across regions, largely influenced by remaining travel restrictions and the strength of domestic tourism. In 2021, tourism had higher economic contributions in Latin America and the Caribbean (5.9 per cent), Northern Africa and Western Asia (5.2 per cent) and Europe and Northern America (2.2 per cent) compared to sub-Saharan Africa (1.2 percent) and Central and Southern Asia (0.4 per cent).

COVID-19 has accelerated the adoption of digital solutions, transforming access to finance

The accelerated adoption of digital solutions, fuelled in part by the COVID-19 pandemic, is transforming access to finance. In 2021, 76 per cent of adults worldwide had an account at a bank or regulated institution such as a credit union, microfinance institution, or mobile money service-provider, a notable increase from 62 per cent in 2014. Technology has played a crucial role in advancing financial inclusion, as evidenced by the sizeable increase in mobile money accounts, from 4 per cent in 2017 to 10 per cent in 2021. New opportunities to reach the unbanked include leveraging digital payments, such as direct transfers of social welfare or wage payments, along with interoperable payments networks and telecommunications infrastructure. During the COVID-19 crisis, 39 per cent of adults in low- and middle-income economies opened their first account at a financial institution specifically to receive wage payments or government transfers.

Industry, innovation and infrastructure

- The manufacturing industry's recovery from the coronavirus disease (COVID-19) pandemic remains incomplete and uneven. Global manufacturing growth slowed down to 3.3 per cent in 2022, from 7.4 per cent in 2021. Progress in least developed countries (LDCs) is far from sufficient to reach the target of doubling the manufacturing share in gross domestic product (GDP) by 2030. However, medium-high- and high-technology industries demonstrated robust growth rates.

- As of 2022, 95 per cent of the world's population was within reach of a mobile broadband network, but some areas remain underserved.

- Global carbon dioxide (CO_2) emissions from energy combustion and industrial processes grew by 0.9 per cent to a new all-time high of 36.8 billion metric tons, well below global GDP growth, reverting to a decade-long trend of decoupling emissions and economic growth.

Workers in Bhutan address Phangyul's water scarcity with the installation of a pressurized piped irrigation scheme, retrofitted with new and climate-resilient technology. The new irrigation will benefit 24 villages and more than 1,300 acres of agricultural land.

- To achieve Goal 9 by 2030, it is essential to support LDCs, invest in advanced technologies, lower carbon emissions and increase mobile broadband access.

Least developed countries face challenges in achieving the manufacturing target by 2030

After rebounding from the COVID-19 pandemic with a 7.4 per cent growth rate in 2021, global manufacturing growth is estimated to have slowed to 3.3 per cent in 2022. This is primarily due to high inflation, energy price shocks, persistent disruptions in the supply of raw materials and intermediate goods, and global economic deceleration. In 2021, global manufacturing employment returned to its pre-pandemic level. However, the share of manufacturing employment in total employment continued to decline worldwide, falling from 14.3 per cent in 2015 to 13.6 per cent in 2021.

Despite the slowdown, the global manufacturing value added (MVA) per capita increased from $1,646 (constant 2015 prices) in 2015 to $1,879 in 2022. Europe and Northern America reached an all-time high of $5,093 in 2022, while the MVA per capita in LDCs reached $159. Although the share of manufacturing as a proportion of GDP in LDCs increased from 12.1 per cent in 2015 to 14.0 per cent in 2022, the pace is insufficient to reach the target of doubling its share by 2030. While LDCs in Asia have made considerable progress, African LDCs would need to change the current trajectory and accelerate progress significantly to attain the target by 2030.

Manufacturing value as a share of GDP in LDCs, 2015–2022 (percentage)

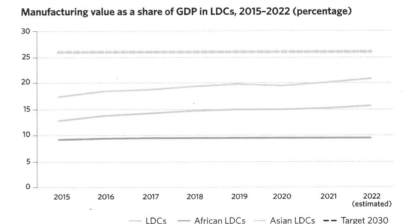

LDCs —— African LDCs —— Asian LDCs – – Target 2030

Economic growth outpaced increases in CO_2 emissions, aided by the use of clean technologies and reduced industrial output

In 2022, global CO_2 emissions from energy combustion and industrial processes grew by 0.9 per cent and reached a record high of 36.8 billion metric tons. After a more than 5 per cent reduction in 2020 during the pandemic, emissions grew over 6 per cent in 2021, surpassing pre-pandemic levels, driven by economic stimulus and a surge in coal demand. The rebound was faster in advanced economies, where aviation emissions reached 85 per cent of 2019 levels, compared with 73 per cent in emerging market and developing economies. CO_2 increases in 2022 were well below global GDP growth of 3.2 per cent, returning to the decade-long trend of decoupling emissions from economic growth, which was disrupted by the sharp rebound in 2021. The increased deployment of clean energy technologies, such as renewables, electric vehicles and heat pumps, and reduced industrial production, particularly in China and Europe, helped

prevent additional emissions, resulting in lower-than-expected global emissions growth.

Global CO_2 emissions from energy combustion and industrial processes, 2000–2022 (billion metric tons)

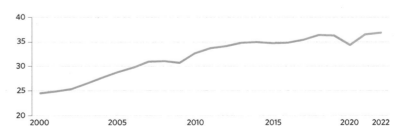

Global research and development spending is up, particularly since the pandemic, but is still too low in least developed countries

Global expenditure on research and development (R&D) as a proportion of GDP increased from 1.69 per cent in 2015 to 1.93 per cent in 2020. The significant increase in 2020 was primarily driven by increased R&D investments and substantial declines in GDP. However, there were gaping regional differences. Europe and Northern America, and Eastern and South-Eastern Asia led the way, spending 2.62 per cent and 2.31 per cent of GDP on R&D in 2020, respectively. But many regions were still spending less than 1 per cent of their GDP on R&D in 2020, such as 0.32 per cent in sub-Saharan Africa to 0.90 per cent in Northern Africa and Western Asia. Meanwhile, LDCs, and landlocked developing countries (LLDCs) were spending around 0.27 per cent and 0.20 per cent of their GDP on R&D, respectively.

The number of researchers per million inhabitants has increased worldwide from 1,022 in 2010 and 1,160 in 2015 to 1,342 in 2020. However, women accounted for only 31.2 per cent of global researchers in 2020. To leverage innovation for post-pandemic recovery and sustainable development, strong policies to spur R&D investment and increase the number of researchers are crucial, particularly in developing economies.

Research and development expenditure as a proportion of GDP, 2015 and 2020 (percentage)

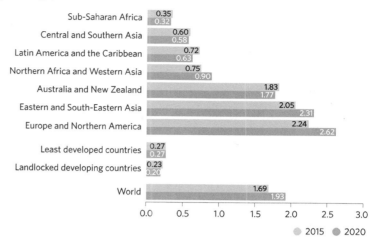

Note: There is insufficient data coverage for Oceania (excluding Australia and New Zealand) to calculate a regional aggregate.

Strong growth in medium-high- and high-technology industries amid global manufacturing slowdown

In 2022, while overall global manufacturing growth slowed, medium-high- and high-technology industries remained strong as a result of a recovery in the automotive sector and consistently strong production of computers, electronics and optical products, and electrical equipment. However, the production of basic pharmaceuticals experienced a loss for the first time in 2022 as the sector readjusted to the COVID-19 situation and faced a shortage of essential inputs.

In 2020, the share of medium-high and high-technology production within total manufacturing remained low in sub-Saharan Africa and LDCs, at 21.7 per cent and 10.6 per cent, respectively, compared with 47.7 per cent in Europe and Northern America and 47.1 per cent in Eastern Asia. Transitioning to medium- and high-tech industry not only holds promise for sustainable economic growth, but also contributes to green growth as these activities are generally less energy- and emission-intensive.

Year-over-year growth rate of global manufacturing production, by technology, fourth quarter of 2019 to fourth quarter of 2022 (percentage)

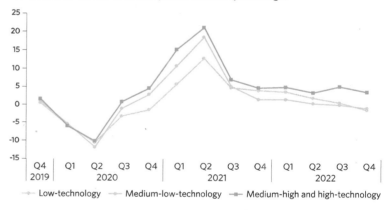

More than 95 per cent of the world has mobile broadband access of at least 3G, but connecting the final frontier is proving difficult

In 2022, mobile broadband coverage of 3G or higher was available to 95 per cent of the global population, a significant increase from 78 per cent in 2015. However, connecting the remaining 5 per cent presents challenges. The coverage gap is 18 per cent in sub-Saharan African and 32 per cent in Oceania.

Between 2015 and 2022, 4G network coverage doubled, reaching 88 per cent of the world's population, but growth has slowed. Currently, coverage exceeds 90 per cent of the population in most regions. Only Latin America and the Caribbean, Northern Africa and Western Asia, Oceania (excluding Australia and New Zealand) and sub-Saharan Africa remain below that threshold. Preliminary data show that in 2021, 19 per cent of the global population was covered by a 5G network. Many countries are phasing out older-generation networks to adopt more efficient networks compatible with 5G. However, in other countries, particularly low-income countries, 2G and 3G networks retain a significant presence, and there are barriers to 5G deployment, including high infrastructure costs, device affordability, and regulatory and adoption constraints.

Proportion of population covered by a mobile network, 2022 (percentage)

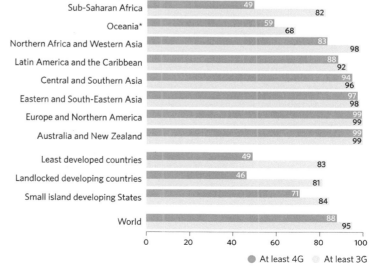

* Excluding Australia and New Zealand.

Reduced inequalities

Migrants cross the dangerous Darien jungle between Colombia and Panama, which saw a seven-fold increase in the number of children going through the jungle in the first two months of 2023 compared with 2022.

- The incomes of the poorest 40 per cent of the population had been growing faster than the national average in most countries. But emerging yet inconclusive evidence suggests that COVID-19 may have put a dent in this positive trend of falling within-country inequality. The pandemic has also caused the largest rise in between-country inequality in three decades.

- One in six people worldwide has experienced discrimination in some form, with women and people with disabilities disproportionately affected.

- The year 2022 witnessed the highest number of refugees (34.6 million people) ever documented. This year is also a deadly one for migrants, with nearly 7,000 deaths recorded globally.

- Reducing both within- and between-country inequality requires equitable resource distribution, investing in education and skills development, implementing social protection measures, combating discrimination, supporting marginalized groups and fostering international cooperation for fair trade and financial systems.

Most countries experienced increased shared prosperity, but the pandemic may have reversed some of this progress

Among countries with data for 2009–2022, more than half achieved income growth for the poorest 40 per cent of the population at a rate higher than the national average. But the share of countries that experienced shared prosperity was higher in high- and middle-income regions than in their fragile and low-income peers. More than three-quarters of countries in Europe and Northern America and 6 out of 10 countries in Eastern and South-Eastern Asia saw the incomes of the poorest 40 per cent grow faster than the national average. However, in Central and Southern Asia and sub-Saharan Africa, the incomes of the poorest 40 per cent grew faster than the mean in only 30–38 per cent of countries.

Post-2019 data are still sparse and inconclusive. In two thirds of the 50 countries with data, the poorest 40 per cent experienced higher income growth than the national average. However, this trend is largely driven by Europe and Northern America where more data are available and where large transfer programmes have mitigated COVID-19's economic impacts on the bottom of the income distribution. Emerging evidence indicates that inequality within countries may have worsened as a result of the pandemic, with surveys in 2021 showing that poorer households lost incomes and jobs at slightly higher rates than richer households.

Share of countries where income growth of the poorest 40 per cent of the population is higher than the national average, 2009–2022 (percentage)

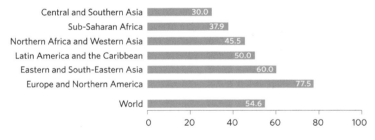

Central and Southern Asia	30.0
Sub-Saharan Africa	37.9
Northern Africa and Western Asia	45.5
Latin America and the Caribbean	50.0
Eastern and South-Eastern Asia	60.0
Europe and Northern America	77.5
World	54.6

The pandemic has caused the largest rise in income inequality between countries in three decades

Over the past three decades, incomes in lower and middle-income countries have been catching up to those of richer countries. Overall, the income differences between countries decreased by 37 per cent between 1990 and 2019. Recently, however, this convergence has slowed considerably. The average annual decline in inequality between countries in the last five years before the pandemic was 0.3 per cent, much lower than the average annual reduction of 1.8 per cent between 1991 and 2014. And although there had been increases in global between-country inequality in only 5 of the 29 years before the pandemic, the onslaught of COVID-19 has caused the largest increase in between-country inequality in three decades, according to World Bank estimates.[3] Between-country inequality is projected to have risen 4.4 per cent between 2019 and 2020, compared with the pre-pandemic forecast of a 0.8 per cent reduction.

Change in inequality between countries, 1990–2020 (percentage)

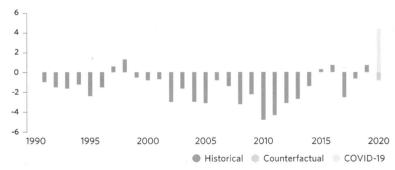

Note: The annual changes in inequality between countries use the mean log deviation.

3   Mahler, Daniel G., Nishant Yonzan and Christoph Lakner, "The Impact of COVID-19 on Global Inequality and Poverty." Policy Research Working Paper, No. 10198 (Washington, D.C., World Bank, 2022).

Racial discrimination is one of the most common grounds for discrimination worldwide

The latest available data show that close to one in six people globally experience discrimination based on any grounds. Among both women and men, racial discrimination, rooted in factors such as ethnicity, colour or language, is among the most common grounds. Discrimination based on age and religion, though slightly less widespread, also affects women and men almost equally. Women are twice as likely as men to report instances of discrimination based on sex and almost twice as likely as men to experience discrimination on the basis of marital status. Persons with disabilities also encounter high levels of discrimination, with one in three reporting such experiences, twice the rate encountered by individuals without disabilities.

Proportion of the overall population experiencing discrimination, by selected grounds and sex, 2015–2022 (percentage)

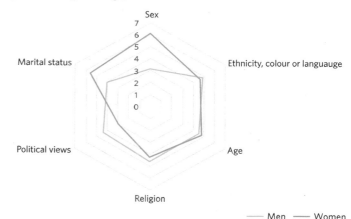

With deaths along migratory routes rising globally, urgent action is needed to ensure safe migration

According to the Missing Migrants Project of the International Organization for Migration (IOM), a total of 56,216 deaths on migratory routes worldwide have been recorded since 2014, of which 6,876 were in 2022 and 2,091 were as of mid-June 2023. With the exception of 2020, more than 5,000 deaths had been documented during migration each year between 2014 and 2022.

In 2022, at least 3,167 people died on maritime and land routes to and through Europe, accounting for more than half of the fatalities recorded worldwide that year. It was also the deadliest year in the Americas and Asia since data collection began, with 1,432 and 1,843 individuals losing their lives during migration, respectively. These data show lack of progress in reducing migrant deaths worldwide since 2015. While there was a decline in deaths during the first year of the pandemic, the numbers have since returned to pre-pandemic levels and in many cases even surpassed them.

Number of deaths during migration, by region, 2022

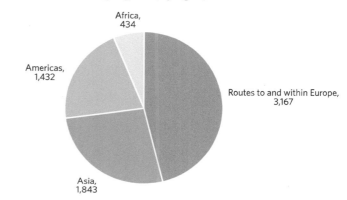

Note: The regions correspond to IOM regional definitions.

Record numbers of people are fleeing their countries in the face of mounting crises

The global number of refugees has increased annually for more than a decade, reaching 34.6 million by the end of 2022, the highest number ever recorded. This represents 429 out of 100,000 people, or 1 in 233, who fled their countries of origin owing to war, conflict, persecution, human rights violations or events seriously disturbing the public order. This represents an increase of more than 100 per cent compared with 2015. Overall, 52 per cent of all refugees and other people in need of international protection came from just three countries: the Syrian Arab Republic (6.5 million), Ukraine (5.7 million) and Afghanistan (5.7 million). Around 41 per cent of all refugees at the end of 2022 were children, while 51 per cent of refugees were women and girls. Low- and middle-income countries hosted 76 per cent of the world's refugees and other people in need of international protection, with the LDCs providing asylum to 20 per cent of the total.

Proportion of the population who are refugees, by region of origin, 2015 and 2022 (per 100,000 population in the region of origin)

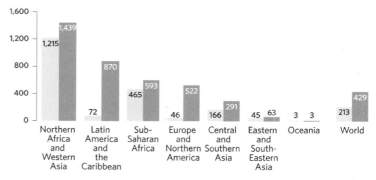

Sustainable cities and communities

A metro line tunnel and station providing a safer and more sustainable transport system is under construction in Lima, Peru.

- Over half of the global population currently resides in urban areas, a rate projected to reach 70 per cent by 2050. Approximately 1.1 billion people currently live in slums or slum-like conditions in cities, with 2 billion more expected in the next 30 years.

- In 2022, only half of the world's urban population had convenient access to public transportation. Urban sprawl, air pollution and limited open public spaces persist in cities.

- Since 2015, the number of countries with national and local disaster risk reduction strategies has doubled.

- To achieve Goal 11, efforts must focus on implementing inclusive, resilient and sustainable urban development policies and practices that prioritize access to basic services, affordable housing, efficient transportation and green spaces for all.

Smaller cities and towns in many regions are recording faster growth in slum populations than major cities

The world's population reached 8 billion in November 2022, with over half (55 per cent) living in urban areas, a figure projected to rise to 70 per cent by 2050. Most of the urban growth is taking place in small cities and intermediate towns, exacerbating inequalities and urban poverty. While the proportion of the urban population living in slums declined slightly, from 25.4 to 24.2 per cent between 2014 and 2020, the total number of slum dwellers continues to rise with increasing urbanization. In 2020, an estimated 1.1 billion urban residents lived in slums or slum-like conditions. Over the next 30 years, an additional 2 billion people are expected to live in such settlements – some 183,000 people daily – mostly in developing countries. Today, 85 per cent of slum dwellers are concentrated in three regions: Central and Southern Asia (359 million), Eastern and South-Eastern Asia (306 million) and sub-Saharan Africa (230 million). The escalating slum population is a manifestation of the housing crisis, highlighting the need for diverse housing options, equitable public transportation and basic services to meet the varied needs of urban residents.

Proportion of global urban population living in slums (percentage) and total slum population (millions), 2000–2020

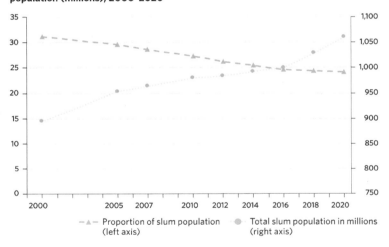

- –▲– Proportion of slum population (left axis)
- ● Total slum population in millions (right axis)

The demand for urban transportation continues to grow exponentially, particularly in developing countries

The quality and availability of transportation infrastructure varies greatly across countries and regions and even within cities. In developed countries, people tend to have more than one transportation option, although these are not always available in an equitable or environmentally sensitive manner. But in the developing world, where an estimated 1 billion people still lack access to all-weather roads, the demand for mobility for people and goods has been expanding exponentially every year. Data from 2022 reveal that only 51.6 per cent of the global urban population has convenient access to public transport, with considerable regional differences. Countries and cities, particularly in the developing world, still have a long way to go in terms of developing safe, affordable, accessible and sustainable transport systems. There is a pressing need for cities worldwide to integrate motorized transportation systems with walking and cycling through long-term sustainable urban mobility plans, targeted infrastructure investments and policy implementation.

Coverage of public transport and share of population with convenient access in urban areas, 2022 (percentage)

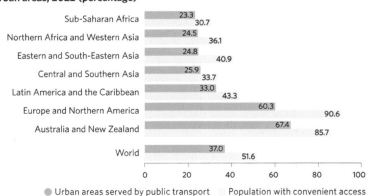

Region	Urban areas served by public transport	Population with convenient access
Sub-Saharan Africa	23.3	30.7
Northern Africa and Western Asia	24.5	36.1
Eastern and South-Eastern Asia	24.8	40.9
Central and Southern Asia	25.9	33.7
Latin America and the Caribbean	33.0	43.3
Europe and Northern America	60.3	90.6
Australia and New Zealand	67.4	85.7
World	37.0	51.6

● Urban areas served by public transport   Population with convenient access

Note: Based on data from 1,507 cities in 126 countries.

Air pollution is not only an urban problem, but is also affecting towns and rural areas

Globally, air quality is improving, largely due to advancements in high-income countries. However, small island developing States (SIDS) are experiencing either stagnant or worsening air quality levels, albeit lower than the global average. To compound matters, air pollution monitoring in these countries is limited or non-existent. Low- and middle-income countries account for only 42 per cent of the 117 countries reporting air pollution data from cities, and SIDS represent a mere 3 per cent of these countries. Although cities have traditionally been the focus of air pollution reduction policies, air quality in towns and rural areas should also be considered. In 2019, towns in Eastern and South-Eastern Asia, a region with a significant proportion of the world's population, experienced poorer air quality than cities. Tackling air pollution requires a shift in perspective, acknowledging that it is not solely an urban issue. While urban areas continue to be important, a comprehensive approach that also considers towns and rural areas is crucial to combat air pollution effectively.

Population-weighted particulate matter (PM$_{2.5}$) concentrations in cities, towns and rural areas, 2019 (micrograms per cubic metre)

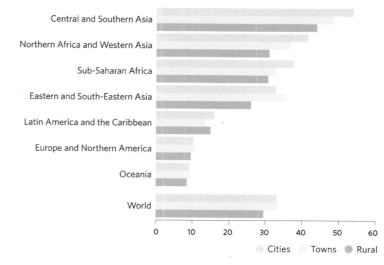

Provision and access to open public spaces remains low across regions, impacting negatively on the quality of urban life

Public spaces enhance inclusion, social cohesion and the productivity of cities. However, 2020 data from 1,072 cities reveal that more than three-quarters have less than 20 per cent of their area dedicated to open public spaces and streets. This figure falls short of the target of 45–50 per cent, of which 15–25 per cent should be open public spaces and 30–35 per cent streets and sidewalks. On average, open public spaces accounted for a mere 3.2 per cent of urban land in 2020, about four times less than the share occupied by streets. However, these figures vary widely across regions, and cities in more developed regions have higher proportions of land dedicated to streets and open spaces than those in developing regions. Furthermore, countries in developed regions also have higher shares of the population with convenient access to open public spaces.

Proportion of cities in each region where the population has access to open public spaces, within a 400-metre walking distance, 2020 (percentage)

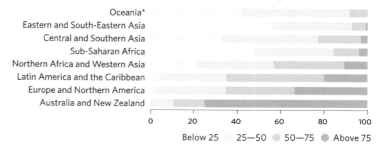

* Excluding Australia and New Zealand.

Urban sprawl is outpacing population growth in most cities, with detrimental effects on sustainability

Data from 681 cities spanning 30 years reveal that the global physical expansion of cities has outpaced population growth. For the period 1990–2000, the global land consumption rate averaged 2.9 per cent, while the population growth rate averaged 2.3 per cent. These rates declined to 2.0 per cent and 1.6 per cent respectively for the period 2000–2010, and further declined to 1.5 per cent and 1.2 per cent respectively in 2010–2020. The overall steady decline in both the population growth rate and land consumption rate was observed in all regions, except Northern Africa and Western Asia, where a higher population growth rate was recorded during the 2000–2010 period than in 1990–2000. The resulting urban sprawl results in cities becoming less dense as they expand, but its unplanned nature has detrimental effects on the sustainability of urban development.

Since 2015, many more national and local governments have reported having disaster risk reduction strategies

The number of countries with national disaster risk reduction strategies has increased from 55 in 2015 to 126 by the end of 2022. One crucial aspect of these strategies is to promote policy coherence and compliance, notably with the SDGs and the Paris Agreement – with 118 countries reporting having some degree of policy coherence. In addition to national efforts, local governments worldwide have also made progress on developing and implementing local disaster risk reduction strategies in line with national strategies. By the end of 2022, a total of 102 countries reported having local governments with disaster risk reduction strategies, a substantial increase from 51 in 2015. Among these countries, the average proportion of local governments that have local disaster risk reduction strategies is 72 per cent.

Responsible consumption and production

- The material footprint per capita in high-income countries is 10 times the level of low-income countries. The world is also seriously off track in its efforts to halve per capita food waste and losses by 2030.

- Global crises triggered a resurgence in fossil fuel subsidies, nearly doubling from 2020 to 2021.

- Reporting has increased on corporate sustainability and on public procurement policies, but has fallen when it comes to sustainable consumption and monitoring sustainable tourism.

- Responsible consumption and production must be integral to recovery from the pandemic and to acceleration plans of the Sustainable Development Goals. It is crucial to implement policies that support a shift towards sustainable practices and decouple economic growth from resource use.

Workers sort plastics at a recycling plant in Côte d'Ivoire. Plastic pollution threatens the country's coast, lagoons, fishing and tourism. Overhauling the economic model governing plastics is essential to address this crisis.

Regional inequalities in material footprints highlight consumption disparities

Between 2000 and 2019, global domestic material consumption (DMC) – the amount of raw materials directly used for production processes in a country – increased by 66 per cent, tripling since the 1970s to reach 95.1 billion metric tons. In 2019, the corresponding material footprint – the amount of materials extracted to satisfy final consumption demand in a country – was 95.9 billion metric tons. While the total volumes are similar globally, comparisons reveal regional inequalities in the environmental impact. In Northern Africa and Western Asia, and in Europe and Northern America, the material footprint in 2019 exceeded DMC by 18 per cent and 14 per cent, respectively, while in Latin America and the Caribbean and sub-Saharan Africa, the material footprint was lower than DMC by 17 per cent and 32 per cent, respectively. These differences highlight the unequal responsibilities and consumption disparities between import-oriented and export-oriented and generally high-income and low-income countries. The material footprint per capita in high-income countries is 10 times the level of low-income countries. Therefore, it is essential to adopt sustainable policies and raise awareness to ensure efficient and sustainable management of limited and unequally exploited natural resources by 2030.

Excess of domestic material consumption over material footprint, 2019 (percentage)

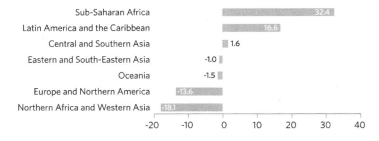

Sub-Saharan Africa	32.4
Latin America and the Caribbean	16.6
Central and Southern Asia	1.6
Eastern and South-Eastern Asia	-1.0
Oceania	-1.5
Europe and Northern America	-13.6
Northern Africa and Western Asia	-18.1

Fossil fuel subsidies rise back to 2014 levels despite calls for a phase-out

Fossil fuel subsidies create distortions in energy markets, hinder the transition to cleaner and more sustainable alternatives, and undermine efforts to combat climate change. In 2021, global data showed a resurgence of such subsidies, with governments spending an estimated $732 billion on subsidies for coal, oil and gas, nearly doubling the $375 billion spent in 2020. This was largely attributed to a rebound in energy prices after a drop in 2020, bringing subsidies back to 2014 levels. Unfortunately, the global energy crisis triggered by Russia's invasion of Ukraine in 2022 is likely to cause another increase in fossil fuel subsidies. Hopefully, these will be short-term measures aimed at protecting consumers from the impacts of the crisis. Many governments are now taking steps towards longer-term solutions. Some are seeking to increase or diversify oil and gas supplies, while others are accelerating structural changes.

Global estimates of fossil fuel subsidies, by fuel type, 2010–2021 (billions of dollars, nominal value)

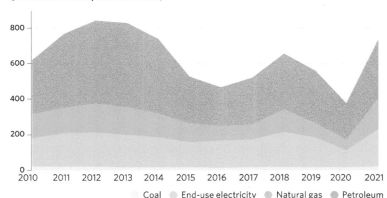

Coal ● End-use electricity ● Natural gas ● Petroleum

Despite rising global hunger, food waste and losses are staggering and uneven

In 2021, although 828 million people were facing hunger, 13.2 per cent of the world's food was lost after harvest along the supply chain from farm to consumer, hardly changed since 2016 and falling short of the target of substantially reducing post-harvest food losses by 2030. An additional 17 per cent of food is wasted at household, food service, and retail levels, resulting in a staggering 931 million tons of food waste or 120 kilograms per capita in 2019. Sub-Saharan Africa experiences the highest food loss, at 20 per cent, compared with 9 per cent in Europe and Northern America. While food loss shows regional differences, especially between high and low-income regions, household food waste per capita is similar across all regional groups, highlighting the need for action in all countries. Despite the importance of reducing food loss and waste, data are still scarce. Tackling food loss and waste is urgent and requires dedicated policies, informed by data, as well as investments in technologies, infrastructure, education and monitoring.

Estimated total food waste and food waste in households per person, 2019 (kilograms)

*Excluding Australia and New Zealand.

More companies, large and small, are reporting on their efforts to improve sustainability

The trend towards sustainability reporting is on the rise, with around 70 per cent of monitored companies publishing sustainability reports in 2021 – triple the percentage since 2016. South-Eastern Asia and Central America have experienced the highest increase in sustainability reporting between 2020 and 2021, while the highest volume of reports is seen in Eastern Asia, Europe and Northern America. While large companies continue to lead the way in sustainability reporting, there is evidence of growth in disclosures among small and medium-sized enterprises, with growth rates of 37 and 34 per cent, respectively, between 2020 and 2021. Companies are most likely to disclose policies related to water and energy, CO_2 emissions, occupational health and safety, and board diversity. Companies continue to detail their activities in attaining the Sustainable Development Goals, but only 10 per cent report on all 17 Goals. Overall, the trend towards better sustainability reporting is a positive development, indicating a growing awareness of the need to prioritize sustainable practices across all industries.

Increase in companies publishing sustainability reports, between 2020 and 2021 (percentage)

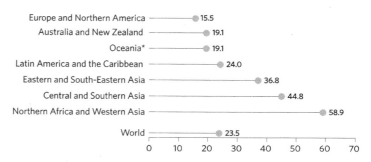

*Excluding Australia and New Zealand.

Global cooperation on sustainable consumption and production rises, while reporting dwindles

Multilateral and multi-stakeholder cooperation on sustainable consumption has increased since 2015, inspiring science-based and transformative policies in numerous countries. Between 2019 and 2022, 485 policy instruments supporting the shift to sustainable consumption and production were reported by 62 countries and the European Union, with increasing linkages to global environmental commitments on climate, biodiversity, pollution, waste and high-impact sectors. Meanwhile, reporting has been decreasing by an average of 30 per cent every year since 2019, and continues to reflect great regional imbalances, with more than 50 per cent of policy instruments reported from Europe and Central Asia. Nevertheless, the international community adopted three ambitious agreements in 2022, including the Sharm el-Sheikh Implementation Plan for a new global climate pact, the Kunming-Montreal Global Biodiversity Framework, and the United Nations Environment Assembly resolution 5/14 on ending plastic pollution. These agreements underscore the need to shift towards a more sustainable and circular approach to consumption and production.

Despite increased public procurement reporting, sustainable tourism monitoring is down

Public procurement is a key factor in the economy of all countries, representing on average 13–20 per cent of GDP. Governments can leverage their purchasing power to drive markets towards greener and more innovative products and services, supporting sustainable development. In 2022, 67 national governments reported to the United Nations Environment Programme on the implementation of sustainable public procurement policies and action plans, a 50 per cent increase from 2020. However, data show a marked decline in the number of countries implementing tools to monitor the sustainable development impacts of tourism in 2020–2021, mainly due to disrupted statistical operations during the COVID-19 pandemic. While tourism contributes to creating jobs and promoting local culture and products, sustainable management of the sector's development is essential to protect its value. Countries must prioritize monitoring sustainable tourism practices as part of their recovery, ensuring economically viable and environmentally sustainable tourism.

Climate action

- With a climate cataclysm looming, the pace and scale of current climate action plans are wholly insufficient to effectively tackle climate change. Increasingly frequent and intense extreme weather events are already impacting every region on Earth. Rising temperatures will escalate these hazards further, posing grave risks.

- The Intergovernmental Panel on Climate Change (IPCC) emphasizes that deep, rapid and sustained reductions in greenhouse gas (GHG) emissions are essential in all sectors, beginning now and continuing throughout this decade. To limit global warming to 1.5°C above pre-industrial levels, emissions must already be decreasing and need to be cut by almost half by 2030, just seven years away.

- Urgent and transformative action is crucial, going beyond mere plans and promises. It requires raising ambition, covering entire economies and moving towards climate-resilient development, while outlining a clear path to achieve net-zero emissions. Time is running out, and immediate measures are necessary to avoid catastrophic consequences and secure a sustainable future for generations to come.

Two men wade through flood water in Pakistan after torrential monsoon rains dumped up to five times the 30-year average rainfall. Such events are now more likely and more severe due to climate change.

Urgent global greenhouse gas emission reductions are needed to avert 1.5°C tipping point

The latest IPCC synthesis report unequivocally states that human activities, particularly over a century of burning fossil fuels, unsustainable energy and land use, and untenable consumption and production patterns, have caused global warming of 1.1°C above pre-industrial levels. This has led to a surge in extreme weather and climate events in every region, which is now the everyday face of climate change. Vulnerable communities, despite having contributed the least to climate change, are disproportionately affected. Between 2010 and 2020, highly vulnerable regions, home to approximately 3.3–3.6 billion people, experienced 15 times higher human mortality rates from floods, droughts and storms compared to regions with very low vulnerability. The adverse impacts of climate change have caused substantial damages and increasingly irreparable losses to ecosystems and human lives, triggering food shortages, loss of housing and infrastructure, migration of populations, and more. With further temperature increases, these extreme events will worsen and become harder to manage. Moreover, the effectiveness of adaptation measures diminishes with heightened warming.

The United Nations Framework Convention on Climate Change (UNFCCC)'s latest nationally determined contributions (NDC) synthesis report finds that the combined climate pledges of 193 Parties under the Paris Agreement will achieve a slight decrease (0.3 per cent) in GHG emissions by 2030 compared to 2019 levels. However, this falls well short of the 43 per cent emissions reduction called for by the IPCC to be on the 1.5°C pathway and would propel the world to an unsustainable potential warming of around 2.5°C by the end of the century.

The IPCC warns that without strengthened cross-sectoral policies, the world is likely to surpass the critical 1.5°C tipping point by 2035. How livable the

world will be for current and future generations will depend on the choices we make today. To curb climate change, rapid, deep and sustained GHG emissions reductions in all sectors, starting now, are vital. This requires global climate-resilient development action, accelerated adaptation and mitigation measures and leveraging SDG synergies. Increased finance, political commitment, coordinated policies, international cooperation, ecosystem stewardship and inclusive governance are all urgently needed for effective and equitable climate action.

Global annual mean temperature relative to pre-industrial levels (1850–1900 average), 1850–2022 (degrees Celsius)

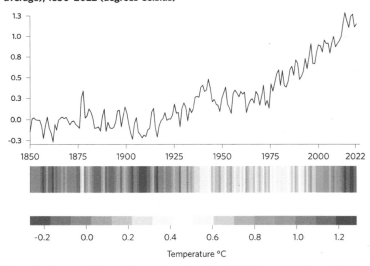

Source: The figure and climate stripes are drawn from the World Meteorological Organization's State of the Global Climate 2022 report, which combines six international data sets for temperature: HadCRUT.5.0.1.0 (UK Met Office), NOAAGlobalTemp v5 (USA), NASA GISTEMP v4 (USA), Berkeley Earth (USA), ERA5 (ECMWF), and JRA-55 (Japan).

Global climate change education has so far not kept up with youth demand

Students and youth globally are demanding climate action and comprehensive and quality climate education to prepare them for a greener future. Nearly all countries (94 per cent) report that climate change education is included in their curricula. However, evidence suggests otherwise. An analysis of national curriculum frameworks in 100 countries reveals that nearly half (47 per cent) do not even mention climate change. While 95 per cent of teachers acknowledge the importance of teaching students about climate change severity, only about one-third can effectively explain the effects of climate change in their region. Furthermore, 70 per cent of youth can, at best, explain only the broad principles of climate change. One in five youth feels unprepared for climate change based on their education and is asking for more information to grasp its complexities. Youth have emphasized the need for interdisciplinary, action-oriented education that is both globally relevant and tailored to local realities, along with adequate teacher support.

Record-setting rising sea levels are a severe threat to hundreds of millions of people

Record-high GHG concentrations are pushing global temperatures higher and trapping heat, with approximately 90 per cent of heat being absorbed by the ocean. This is causing sea levels to rise through ice loss on land, melting glaciers and ice sheets, and thermal expansion. According to the World Meteorological Organization, global average sea levels have risen faster since 1900 than in any preceding century over the past 3,000 years. Sea levels continued to rise in 2022, reaching a new record since satellite measurements in 1993. Moreover, the rate of global mean sea-level rise has doubled in the past decade – from 2.27 mm per year in 1993–2002 to 4.62 mm per year in 2013–2022.

Even with efforts to limit warming to 1.5°C, global sea levels are expected to continue rising over the coming century, creating significant hazards for communities worldwide. Small island developing States and low-lying urban areas are particularly vulnerable, facing profound risks to coastal ecosystems and ecosystem services, economies, livelihoods, health and well-being. Around 900 million people live in coastal zones at low elevations, equivalent to 1 in 10 people worldwide. The effects of sea-level rise and other climate impacts are already forcing relocations in countries like Fiji, Vanuatu, the Solomon Islands and elsewhere. Tuvalu even plans to create a digital version of the island to replicate landmarks and preserve its history and culture before it succumbs to rising seas.

Global mean sea level, 1993–2022 (millimetres)

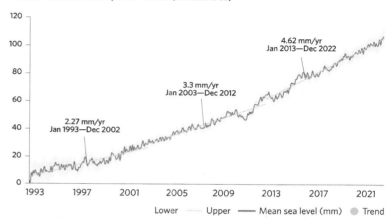

Note: Based on satellite measurements.

Source: Laboratoire d'Etudes en Géophysique et Océanographie Spatiales (LEGOS); data from AVISO altimetry (www.aviso. altimetry.fr). Taken from the World Meteorological Organization's State of the Global Climate 2022 report.

The $100-billion-a-year climate finance goal by developed countries has yet to be met

Climate finance is critical to addressing the climate crisis. According to the UNFCCC, global climate finance flows reached an annual average of $803 billion in 2019–2020, a 12 per cent increase compared with 2017–2018. This growth is attributed to increasing mitigation actions in buildings, infrastructure and transport, as well as increased adaptation finance. However, despite the increase over the last decade, climate finance falls short of the levels needed to limit warming. There is also an uneven distribution of finance across regions. Furthermore, fossil-fuel-related flows exceeded climate financing for adaptation and mitigation in 2020.

According to a recent UNFCCC analysis, developing countries' needs amount to nearly $6 trillion by 2030 to meet their NDCs. The United Nations Environment Programme estimates that adaptation costs alone could reach up to $330 billion per year by 2030.

The commitment of developed countries to mobilize $100 billion in climate finance annually by 2020 through to 2025 has not yet been met. According to an Organisation for Economic Co-operation and Development report, developed countries provided and mobilized a total of $83.3 billion in climate financing for developing countries in 2020, a 4 per cent increase from 2019 but still shy of the target. Furthermore, more than 70 per cent of climate finance by developed countries to developing nations between 2016–2020 was in the form of loans.

The establishment of the Loss and Damage Fund at the 2022 United Nations Climate Conference (COP 27) to provide financial support to the countries most affected by climate change impacts is the most recent step in improving the channels of financial support to respond to the climate challenge. Reconstructing climate finance delivery schemes and designing a new climate finance goal in 2024 are the next milestones to urgently improve both the quantity and the quality of climate finance going forward.

Global climate finance flows, by sector, 2017-2020 (billions of US dollars)

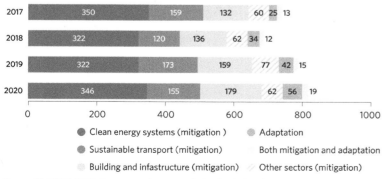

Source: UNFCCC. 2022. *Summary and recommendations by the Standing Committee on Finance: Fifth Biennial Assessment and Overview of Climate Finance Flows*, Bonn: UNFCCC.

Life below water

- The ocean is in a state of emergency as increasing eutrophication, acidification, ocean warming and plastic pollution worsen its health. Additionally, the alarming trend of overfishing persists, leading to the depletion of over one third of global fish stocks.

- While there has been some progress in expanding marine protected areas, combating illegal, unreported and unregulated fishing, banning fishing subsidies and supporting small-scale fishers, action is not advancing at the speed or scale required to meet Goal 14.

- To counter these trends, swift and coordinated global action is imperative. This entails increasing funding for ocean science, intensifying conservation efforts, advancing nature- and ecosystem-based solutions, addressing the interconnections and impacts of human-induced pressures, and urgently turning the tide on climate change to safeguard the planet's largest ecosystem.

An elderly woman plants mangroves in Timor-Leste. Mangroves build shoreline resilience, providing natural protection against erosion and absorbing storm surges, protecting local communities and their livelihoods.

Citizen science sheds light on the magnitude of ocean plastic pollution

Plastic is the most harmful type of marine litter, with over 17 million metric tons clogging the ocean in 2021, a figure set to double or triple by 2040. Plastic production has skyrocketed fourfold in the last 40 years, while recycling rates remain below 10 per cent. This has led to a ubiquitous presence of plastic debris in all ocean habitats, including in fragile Arctic Ocean ice. To gauge the extent of this environmental crisis, one valuable approach is to measure plastic beach litter density. Citizen science initiatives, relying on public volunteers gathering data during beach clean-ups, provide crucial qualitative and quantitative insights to bridge monitoring gaps. Over the last decade, there has been a rise in marine litter-related citizen science initiatives, with many using mobile phone applications to gather and post data. Standardized protocols and improved monitoring systems are also being developed to enhance global efforts to address this pressing issue.

**Selection of beach litter citizen science initiatives, 2023
(coverage, frequency and data collection method)**

	Coverage	Frequency	Data collection method
National Oceanic and Atmospheric Administration Marine Debris Monitoring and Assessment Project (MDMAP)	US west coast, worldwide		🗒
Marine Debris Tracker (formerly part of MDMAP)	Worldwide	●	📱
Ocean Conservancy Trash Information and Data for Education and Solution (TIDES) and Clean Swell app	Worldwide	⊠ ●	📱
Coastal Observation and Seabird Survey Team – Marine Debris	United States		🗒
Australian Marine Debris Initiative Database	Pacific, Oceania	●	📱
Marine LitterWatch	European waters	●	📱

⊠ Annual clean-up   📱 Mobile app
Monthly surveys
● Ongoing clean-ups   🗒 Data sheets

Note: "Ongoing clean-ups" are volunteer-led and ad hoc.

Coastal eutrophication: a growing threat to marine ecosystems and communities

Agriculture, aquaculture and wastewater practices are contributing to nutrient loading in coastal areas, causing widespread coastal eutrophication and algal blooms. These blooms lead to oxygen depletion, harm marine life, contaminate seafood, and damage seagrass and coral reefs, among other impacts. The consequences are severe for marine ecosystem health, local communities, fisheries and tourism. Satellite imagery reveals elevated coastal eutrophication trends globally in 2022 (above the 2000–2004 baseline), though different in magnitude from recent years. Consistently high rates were found in the Arabian Sea, where blooms posed threats to fisheries, tourism and desalination plants, particularly during late winter and early spring, from 2018 to 2022.

In a striking signal of an ocean that can't breathe, crustaceans, such as crawfish and lobster, have been observed leaving the sea to survive. A recent walkout in early 2023 in South Africa saw around 5 tons of endangered lobster escaping, prompting an emergency plan for their rehabilitation in an already struggling fishing community. While blooms can sprout due to natural processes, such as the upwelling of nutrient-rich waters or low-flow waters, human activities are the main driver behind their increasing frequency, duration and expansion. With the added challenge of climate change and its complex interactions with a warming ocean, the impacts of eutrophication on coastal communities are expected to worsen.

Expanding global ocean acidification monitoring is crucial to confront an unabating crisis

As greenhouse gas emissions soar, the oceans are silently absorbing a quarter of annual carbon dioxide emissions. While this mitigates the impact of climate change on the planet, it comes at a great cost to the careful balance in ocean acidity, damaging organisms and ecosystems. Long-term observation sites in the open ocean have shown a continuous decline in pH levels over the last 20 to 30 years, with far-reaching impacts. Currently, the ocean's average pH is 8.1, about 30 per cent more acidic than in pre-industrial times and changing rapidly. Ocean acidification threatens the survival of marine life, disrupts the food web, and undermines vital services provided by the ocean and our own food security. Moreover, this phenomenon weakens and destroys corals and shoreline defenses, degrades habitats and endangers fisheries, aquaculture and tourism. Increased acidification also reduces the ocean's ability to absorb CO_2 and to mitigate climate change.

The number of stations reporting ocean acidification data worldwide has tripled in recent years – from 178 stations in 2021 to 539 in 2023 – providing clearer insights. Nevertheless, data gaps remain in coastal Asia and Africa and the open waters of the South Atlantic, Pacific, Indian and Southern Ocean. Continuous efforts to build capacity to measure and report on ocean acidification, particularly in undersampled areas, are crucial to reducing the local, regional and global impacts of this phenomenon.

Calculated surface pH values based on based on representative sampling stations, 2005-2022 (pH total)

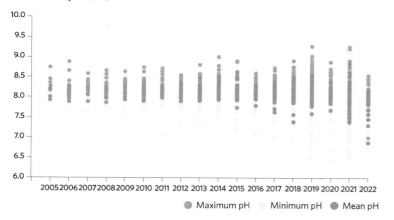

Surface ocean carbonate chemistry measurement locations, 2023 (data-reporting countries and sampling stations)

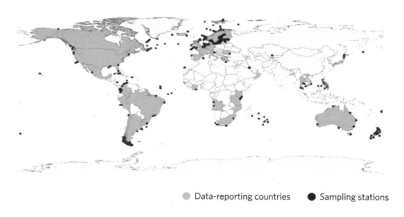

Despite improvements, stronger global cooperation is needed to reel in illegal fishing

Globally, an estimated one in five fish caught originates from illegal, unreported and unregulated (IUU) fishing. This illicit practice is one of the greatest threats to marine ecosystems and fishing communities, distorting competition, undermining legitimate fishers, and devastating marine ecosystems and efforts to conserve marine biodiversity and sustainably manage fish stocks. Annual losses as a result of this practice are estimated at 11 to 26 million tons of fish, with an economic value of up to $23 billion.

IUU fishing can be found in all types of fishing operations and takes place not only in national jurisdiction waters, but also on the high seas. A key instrument to combat IUU fishing is the Agreement on Port State Measures. As of May 2023, the agreement had tripled its signatories since 2016 to reach 75 Parties, including the European Union, to effectively cover 101 States and 60 per cent of port States. Between 2018 and 2022, there has been some progress at the global level in implementing instruments to combat IUU fishing. However, more concerted efforts are needed to ensure greater cooperation among all actors, from "sea to plate", and more transparency and compliance with the international framework, along with strong legislation and greater monitoring and enforcement.

Turning the tide: Recent marine agreements show promise for ocean protection

The global community has reinvigorated its commitment to combat destructive patterns affecting ocean health through several recent pacts. In March 2023, a historic agreement was reached on protecting marine biodiversity in international waters – referred to as the High Seas Treaty – after nearly two decades of negotiations. Given that the "high seas" make up two thirds of the ocean, this treaty, once ratified by countries, will help to provide vital protection against pollution, overfishing and habitat destruction in these critical areas. Another significant milestone occurred in March 2022, when Member States endorsed a resolution to end plastic pollution, including in marine environments, with plans to implement an international legally binding agreement by 2024. The adoption of the World Trade Organization Agreement on Fisheries Subsidies in June 2022 furthered ocean sustainability by banning harmful fisheries subsidies that have contributed to the depletion of the world's fish stocks. Moreover, the United Nations Ocean Conference in June 2022 saw more than 100 Member States voluntarily commit to conserve or protect at least 30 per cent of the global ocean within marine protected areas and implement other effective area-based conservation measures by 2030. These collective efforts demonstrate a renewed determination to revitalize our oceans and ensure a sustainable future for marine ecosystems and communities worldwide.

15 LIFE ON LAND

Life on land

- Terrestrial ecosystems are vital for sustaining human life, contributing to over half of global GDP and encompassing diverse cultural, spiritual, and economic values.

- However, the world faces a triple crisis of climate change, pollution and biodiversity loss. Escalating trends of forest loss, land degradation and the extinction of species pose a severe threat to both the planet and people.

- Despite some progress in sustainable forest management, protected areas, and the uptake of national biodiversity values and natural capital accounting, most improvements have been modest. The recently adopted Kunming-Montreal Global Biodiversity Framework provides renewed impetus for Goal 15, outlining four outcome-oriented goals to be achieved by 2050 and 23 targets to be achieved by 2030.

Villagers in China's eastern Yunhe County revive hillside farms with eco-friendly practices, attracting global visitors and earning recognition as a top ecotourism destination for the restoration of its ecosystem.

- To fulfil Goal 15, a fundamental shift in humanity's relationship with nature is essential, along with accelerated action to address the root causes of these interconnected crises and better recognition of the tremendous value of nature.

Deforestation and forest degradation remain major global threats

Forests are among the largest carbon and biodiversity reservoirs on Earth, crucial for mitigating climate change and providing essential goods, services and livelihoods. However, nearly 100 million hectares of net forest area have been lost over the past two decades. Global forest coverage decreased from 31.9 per cent in 2000 (4.2 billion hectares) to 31.2 per cent (4.1 billion hectares) in 2020. Agricultural expansion is the direct driver of almost 90 per cent of global deforestation (cropland accounts for 49.6 per cent and livestock grazing for 38.5 per cent). Oil palm harvesting alone accounted for 7 per cent of global deforestation from 2000 to 2018.

Agriculture consumed large forested areas in many countries across Latin America, the Caribbean, sub-Saharan Africa and South-East Asia between 2015 and 2020. Conversely, many countries in Asia, Europe and Northern America maintained or increased their forest area over the same period. Global and regional efforts to sustain forest ecosystems as well as their social, economic and environmental functions are essential, in particular for developing countries and the tropics.

Trend in forest area as a proportion of total land area, 2015–2020

● Improvement   Slight or no improvement   ● Slight deterioration
● Deterioration   Insufficient data

Note: Trend categories are based on thresholds for the compound annual growth rate between 2015 and 2020 as follows: Improvement: CAGR > 0.001; Slight or no improvement: $-0.0005 \leq CAGR \leq 0.001$; Slight deterioration: $-0.001 \leq CAGR < -0.0005$; Deterioration: CAGR < -0.001.

Despite efforts to mobilize financing for biodiversity conservation, a persistent funding gap remains

Halting and reversing biodiversity loss requires a comprehensive approach combining regulatory and voluntary measures, while mobilizing and aligning financing for biodiversity. Economic instruments play a crucial role in incentivizing the conservation and sustainable use of biodiversity – and can serve to mobilize finance and mainstream biodiversity across sectors. They include policy instruments such as biodiversity-related taxes, fees and charges, positive subsidies, payments for ecosystem services and biodiversity offsets. ODA is another source of financing for biodiversity.

Between 2017 and 2019, the Organisation for Economic Co-operation and Development (OECD) reported that 234 biodiversity-related taxes in 62 countries generated $8.9 billion annually and payments for environmental

services in 10 countries mobilized $10.1 billion per year. In 2021, ODA in support of biodiversity increased by 26.2 per cent from $7.7 billion (constant 2021 prices) in 2020 to $9.8 billion. This rise can be attributed to international commitments such as the Aichi target on development finance, the recognition of the links between infectious diseases and ecosystem destruction in light of the COVID-19 pandemic, and the parallel focus on addressing climate change and biodiversity loss. But despite progress, there remains a persistent funding gap for biodiversity conservation, emphasizing the need to scale up the use and ambition of economic instruments to protect biodiversity.

Species extinction risk has accelerated each decade since 1993

Plant and animal species are vital for our existence, from pollinating one third of global crops to providing medicines and economic opportunities. Yet, despite this importance, the world is currently facing the largest extinction event since the dinosaurs disappeared. Habitat destruction, invasive species, overexploitation, illegal wildlife trade, pollution and climate change are propelling this crisis. The Red List Index, which measures species' extinction risk across mammal, bird, amphibian, coral and cycad species, has deteriorated by about 11 per cent since 1993, with an accelerating decline each decade. Central and Southern Asia, Eastern and South-Eastern Asia, and Oceania have suffered the fastest declines.

In 2022, assessments revealed that 21 per cent of reptile species are threatened, including the iconic Komodo Dragon in Indonesia, highly valued for ecotourism but endangered by climate change and deforestation. Based on the International Union for Conservation of Nature (IUCN) Red List, it is estimated that 1 million species globally may be threatened with extinction. Urgent action is imperative to halt these potential losses, as they would have irreversible and profound impacts on nature and pose a serious threat to human well-being.

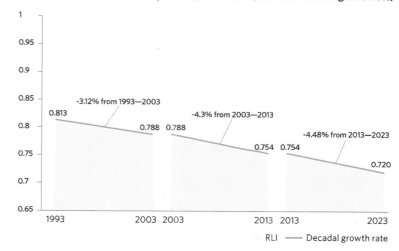

Red List Index rate of decline, by decade, 1993-2023 (Red List index and growth rate)

Growth in protected area coverage of key biodiversity areas has largely stalled

Key biodiversity areas (KBAs) – areas of exceptional importance for species and ecosystems – are crucial for conservation and sustainable development. There are more than 16,000 KBAs globally, and since 2000, the average coverage of KBAs by protected areas has nearly doubled across marine, terrestrial, freshwater and mountain ecosystems. However, progress has largely stagnated since 2015, with uneven growth across regions. The Europe and Northern America region has more than half of its KBAs covered by protected areas, while Central Asia, Southern Asia, Western Asia, Northern Africa, and Oceania all have relatively low coverage. The recently adopted Kunming-Montreal Global Biodiversity Framework represents a new political commitment providing impetus to increase the protected area coverage of KBAs to help safeguard the most significant natural habitats on our planet.

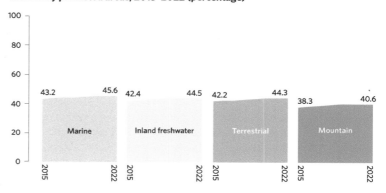

Mean proportion of marine, inland freshwater, terrestrial and mountain KBAs covered by protected areas, 2015–2022 (percentage)

Alarming trends in land degradation call for urgent action to restore the Earth

Between 2015 and 2019, at least 100 million hectares of healthy and productive land were degraded every year, affecting food and water security globally. The loss is equivalent to twice the size of Greenland, impacting the lives of 1.3 billion people, who are estimated to be directly exposed to land degradation. Human activities like urban expansion, deforestation and grassland conversion, coupled with climate change are direct drivers of land degradation worldwide. Demographic and economic trends, governance challenges, and technology and investment gaps also contribute indirectly.

Sub-Saharan Africa, Western Asia, Latin America and the Caribbean, and Southern Asia experienced land degradation at rates faster than the global average. If current trends continue, restoring 1.5 billion hectares of land by 2030 will be necessary to achieve a land-degradation-neutral world. Alternatively, halting any new land degradation and accelerating existing commitments to restore 1 billion hectares can surpass the neutrality target. Land and ecosystem restoration offer cost-effective solutions to address climate change, biodiversity loss, food and water security, and disaster impacts. To this end, governments, businesses and communities must collaborate to conserve natural areas, scale up nature-positive food production and develop green urban areas, infrastructure and supply chains.

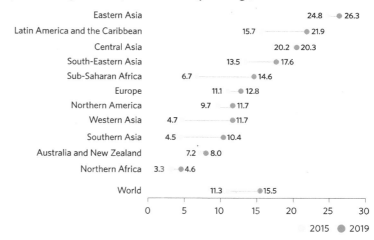

Proportion of degraded land, 2015 and 2019 (percentage)

Note: Regions and subregions may not include all countries.

Peace, justice and strong institutions

- Ongoing and new violent conflicts around the world are derailing the global path to peace and achievement of Goal 16. Alarmingly, the year 2022 witnessed a more than 50 per cent increase in conflict-related civilian deaths, largely due to the war in Ukraine.

- As of the end of 2022, 108.4 million people were forcibly displaced worldwide – an increase of 19 million compared with the end of 2021 and two and a half times the number of a decade ago.

- In 2021, the world experienced the highest number of intentional homicides in the past two decades.

- Structural injustices, inequalities and emerging human rights challenges are putting peaceful and inclusive societies further out of reach. To meet Goal 16 by 2030, action is needed to restore trust and to strengthen the

Shukri, the youngest member of Somalia's first all-women media team, Bilan Media, films in Mogadishu amid the daily threat of targeted violence against journalists.

capacity of institutions to secure justice for all and facilitate peaceful transitions to sustainable development.

Global homicides hit a 20-year high amid escalating gang and sociopolitical violence

Intentional homicides cause more deaths globally than conflict and terrorist killings combined. In 2021, there were approximately 458,000 intentional homicides – the highest number in the past two decades. The noticeable spike in killings in 2021 can be partly attributed to the economic repercussions of COVID-related restrictions, as well as an escalation of gang-related and sociopolitical violence in several countries. Taking the growing population into account, the homicide rate was 5.8 per 100,000 population in 2021, marginally lower than the 2015 rate of 5.9 per 100,000. Even assuming that 2021 has no bearing on future trends, projections based on 2015–2020 suggest that the homicide rate will have fallen by just 24 per cent by 2030 compared with 2015, far short of the target of halving 2015 levels.

In 2021, men and boys accounted for 81 per cent of all homicide victims globally, with a rate four times higher than that of women and girls. Regions with high overall levels of homicidal violence, such as Latin America and the Caribbean and sub-Saharan Africa, record higher shares of male homicide victims than other regions. Additionally, data from 101 countries reveal that more than 9 in 10 suspects of intentional homicides are men or boys.

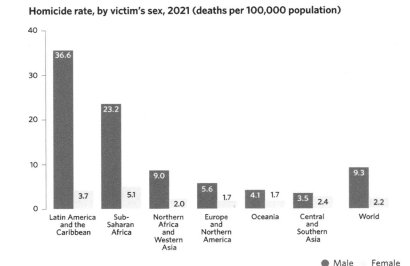

Homicide rate, by victim's sex, 2021 (deaths per 100,000 population)

There has been an unprecedented increase in civilian deaths in conflicts – the first since the adoption of the 2030 Agenda

Civilian deaths directly related to 12 of the world's deadliest conflicts increased by 53 per cent between 2021 and 2022, marking the first rise since the adoption of the 2030 Agenda in 2015. At least 16,988 civilians were killed, with one in five victims being women. The use of heavy weapons and explosive munitions, including indiscriminate and disproportionate attacks, rose from 13 per cent in 2021 to 39 per cent in 2022, signaling a shift in conflict dynamics. Sub-Saharan Africa and Europe accounted for 90 per cent of the deaths, with 4 in 10 occurring specifically in Ukraine. While there was a 23 per cent increase in conflict-related casualties in sub-Saharan Africa, other parts of the world also saw increases in deadly incidents against civilians. These shocking figures demand a renewed global commitment to peace and security, with all parties involved in conflicts urged to abide by international humanitarian and human rights law to protect the lives of civilians, particularly those of children and women.

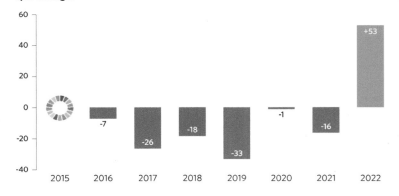

Change in documented conflict-related deaths of civilians, 2015–2022, (percentage)

Falling detection of victims of human trafficking during crises prompts new methods to track and combat this hidden crime

Trafficking in persons is a hidden crime. Available data capture only the number of detected victims, leaving many more unassisted and invisible to authorities. Between 2017 and 2020, data from 141 countries revealed 187,915 detected victims of trafficking. Moreover, in 2020, the number of victims of trafficking detected worldwide fell for the first time in 20 years, a decrease of 11 per cent from 2019. This decline can be attributed to the impact of COVID-19 preventive measures, which altered the dynamics of exploitation and compromised the anti-trafficking response. One emerging result is the 24 per cent drop in the detection of victims of trafficking for sexual exploitation between 2019 and 2020. This is the result of victims exploited in more concealed and dangerous locations. As more victims are likely remaining undetected, increasing efforts are needed to tailor the response to the real prevalence of the crime. Some Member States have shown promising results in testing and implementing new methodologies for prevalence estimates of trafficking in persons.

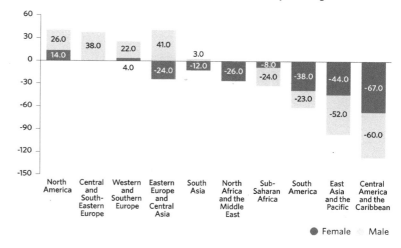

Change in the number of detected victims of trafficking in persons, by sex, per 100,000 population, comparison from 2019 to 2020 (percentage)

● Female   Male

The global prison population keeps rising, creating overcrowding and concerns over the proportion of unsentenced detainees

Access to justice is a fundamental human right for which reducing the number of unsentenced detainees is crucial. After rising steadily from 2015 to 2019, the global prison population declined in 2020 due to COVID-19. Then in 2021, the number of prisoners returned to an upward trend, totalling 11.2 million, with about one-third (3.4 million) held in pre-trial detention. Central and Southern Asia has the highest percentage of unsentenced detainees (60 per cent), while Northern Africa and Western Asia have the lowest (21 per cent). While the overall share remained around 30 per cent from 2015 to 2021, Oceania saw an increase in the share of individuals awaiting trial or sentencing, and Latin America and the Caribbean saw a decrease.

Although prison capacity increased by 19 per cent from 2015 to 2021, overcrowding remains a challenge. Almost half of countries with relevant data (46 out of 96) reported operating at over 100 per cent of their intended capacity, and 18 per cent were functioning at over 150 per cent. Overcrowding adversely affects prisoner health and survival. The data suggest the need for countries to provide adequate space and resources for prisoners to promote rehabilitation, reduce recidivism, and ensure prisoner and societal well-being.

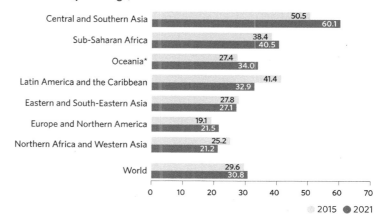

Unsentenced detainees as a proportion of overall prison population, 2015 and 2021 (percentage)

● 2015 ● 2021

* Excluding Australia and New Zealand.

Drug trafficking is generating illicit financial flows worth billions, fuelling corruption and diverting resources

Illicit financial flows fuel corruption and divert criminal proceeds into legal and illegal economic activities. Drug trafficking is a major source of inward and outward illicit financial flows, particularly in countries affected by cross-border drug flows. Recent estimates reveal that Mexican drug cartels alone generated average inward illicit financial flows of $12.1 billion annually between 2015 and 2018, comparable to the value of the country's agricultural exports. Afghanistan, Colombia, Myanmar and Peru also experienced billions of dollars of illicit financial flows from cocaine and opiates trafficking. Opiates trafficking in Asia creates spillover effects, leading to outward illicit financial flows in neighbouring countries. Measuring the value of these illicit financial flows is vital to understanding the motivations behind illegal activities and to developing effective policies to combat them.

The number of young parliamentarians remains low, with few holding leadership positions

In every region of the world except Europe, people under the age of 45 are significantly underrepresented in parliament, relative to their share of national populations. Although the average eligible age to serve in parliament is 23 years, the proportion of members of parliament (MPs) aged 30 and under has remained at about 2–2.6 per cent for the past five years. While the global median age is just over 30 years, the average age of an MP is 51 years. Young MPs hold limited leadership positions, with less than 9 per cent serving as speaker and 17.4 per cent as committee chairs. To increase the participation of younger parliamentarians, efforts must include introducing quotas or lowering the age of eligibility.

Partnerships for the Goals

An Eduardo Kobra mural at United Nations Headquarters in New York, donated by Brazil's Permanent Mission, portrays sustainable development: balancing present needs without compromising the Earth's ability to meet future generations' needs.

- Developing countries are grappling with an unprecedented rise in external debt levels following the COVID-19 pandemic, compounded by challenges such as record inflation, escalating interest rates, competing priorities and constrained fiscal capacity, underscoring the urgent need for debt relief and financial assistance.

- While official development assistance (ODA) flows continue to reach record peaks, the increase in 2022 is primarily attributed to spending on refugees in donor countries and aid to Ukraine.

- Despite a 65 per cent improvement in Internet access since 2015, progress in bridging the digital divide has slowed down post-pandemic. Sustained efforts are required to ensure equitable access to the Internet for all.

- Geopolitical tensions and the resurgence of nationalism hinder international cooperation and coordination, highlighting the importance of a collective surge in action to provide developing countries with the necessary financing and technologies to accelerate the implementation of the SDGs.

In the wake of the pandemic, many developing countries are facing a debt crisis

The debt levels of many countries reached record highs during the pandemic, posing a potential threat to economic growth. The total external debt of low- and middle-income countries reached $9 trillion in 2021, recording a 5.6 per cent increase from 2020. The rise was primarily driven by an increase in short-term debt. Close to 7 in 10 countries in LDCs and LLDCs experienced a higher debt-to-export ratio in 2021 compared with 2015.

Moreover, challenges such as high inflation, competing priorities and rising borrowing costs have exacerbated the risk of debt distress. As of November 2022, more than half (37 out of 69) of the world's poorest countries were either at high risk of, or already in, debt distress. Meanwhile, one in four middle-income countries, home to the majority of the extreme poor, faced a high risk of fiscal crisis. Some countries with unsustainable levels of debt service have already opted for sovereign debt restructuring, while others remain vulnerable.

Debt service as a proportion of exports of goods and services, 2015, 2020 and 2021 (percentage)

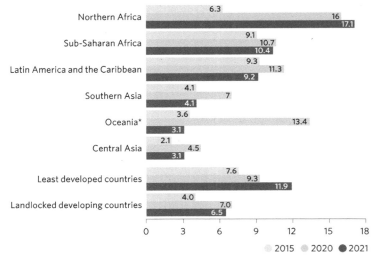

	2015	2020	2021
Northern Africa	6.3	16	17.1
Sub-Saharan Africa	9.1	10.7	10.4
Latin America and the Caribbean	9.3	11.3	9.2
Southern Asia	4.1	7	4.1
Oceania*	3.6	13.4	3.1
Central Asia	2.1	4.5	3.1
Least developed countries	7.6	9.3	11.9
Landlocked developing countries	4.0	7.0	6.5

* Excluding Australia and New Zealand.

Despite record-breaking global trade increases, the share of exports from least developed countries has stagnated and is far off target

Exports of merchandise and services were already slowing down in 2019, but 2020 saw a decline comparable to the recession of 2009. As pandemic-related restrictions were gradually lifted, global exports increased sharply, by 24.8 per cent in 2021 and 12.3 per cent in 2022. Global trade reached a record $32 trillion in 2022. Trade in goods accounted for about $25 trillion (an increase of about 11.5 per cent from 2021) and trade in services totalled about $7 trillion (an increase of about 15.3 per cent from 2021). However, the outlook for global trade in 2023 appears subdued, as a result of deteriorating economic conditions.

The share of exports from LDCs in global merchandise trade was merely 1.1 per cent in 2022, only a 0.07-percentage-point increase from 2021. The target of doubling the share of LDCs' exports by 2020, from its value of 1.02 per cent in 2011, has therefore not been met. On the other hand, all developing countries combined saw an increase in their share of global merchandise trade, reaching 45.3 per cent in 2022, a rise of 4 percentage points compared with 2016. This upward trend has been sustained over the past six years.

Official development assistance surged in 2022 owing to spending on refugees in donor countries and aid to Ukraine

In 2022, net ODA flows by member countries of the Development Assistance Committee (DAC) reached $206 billion (current price), marking an increase of 15.3 per cent in real terms from 2021.[4] This was the fourth consecutive year ODA surpassed its record levels, and one of the highest growth rates recorded in its history. However, total ODA as a percentage of gross national income continues to remain below the target of 0.7 per cent, reaching 0.37 per cent in 2022.

The increase was primarily due to domestic spending on refugees and aid for Ukraine. Refugee costs in donor countries amounted to $29.3 billion in 2022, representing 14.2 per cent of DAC member countries' total ODA. Net ODA to Ukraine accounted for $16.1 billion, representing 7.8 per cent of total ODA. Initial estimates indicate that DAC countries spent $11.2 billion on activities related to COVID-19, down by 45 per cent compared with 2021. Net bilateral ODA flows to African countries experienced a real-term decline of 7.4 per cent compared with 2021.

Components of net ODA, preliminary data, 2022 (current dollars)

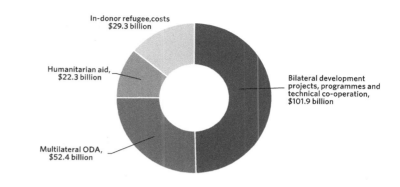

In-donor refugee costs $29.3 billion
Humanitarian aid, $22.3 billion
Bilateral development projects, programmes and technical co-operation, $101.9 billion
Multilateral ODA, $52.4 billion

Internet usage reaches two-thirds of the world's population, but gender and connectivity gaps persist

An estimated 5.3 billion people – 66 per cent of the world's population – used the Internet in 2022. This reflects a substantial increase of 65 per cent from the 40 per cent coverage observed in 2015. The growth rate was 6.1 per cent over 2021, but it falls short of the 11 per cent growth witnessed during the initial stages of the COVID-19 pandemic in 2019–2020. Nevertheless, 2.7 billion people are still offline, highlighting that substantial work is still needed to achieve the universal connectivity target by 2030. Universal connectivity remains particularly challenging in LDCs and LLDCs, where only 36 per cent of the population is currently online.

Globally, 69 per cent of men are using the Internet, compared with 63 per cent of women. This means there were 259 million more male Internet users than female users in 2022.

Proportion of individuals using the Internet, 2015 and 2022 (percentage)

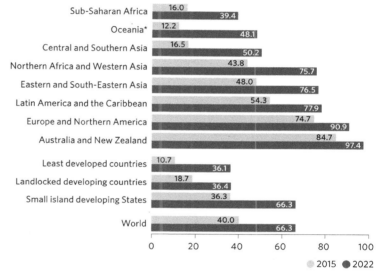

* Excluding Australia and New Zealand.

The world needs more timely, detailed and accurate data to tackle a multitude of crises, but funding for data and statistics is ever more scarce

International funding for data and statistics amounted to only $541 million in 2020, a decrease of more than $100 million and $138 million from funding levels in 2019 and 2018, respectively. Between 2018 and 2020, ODA funding for data dropped by more than 20 per cent. The reduced funding for statistics may impact the most vulnerable countries disproportionately. While data showed international funding bounced back to an estimated amount of $693 million in 2021, this increase was mainly due to one donor, and total funding remained insufficient to meet the growing need for more and better data. Countries still face long-standing challenges in mainstreaming data activities, with a limited pool of donors and low strategic priority generally assigned to statistics.

A total of 156 countries and territories were implementing a national statistical plan in 2022, up from 150 in 2021, with 100 of these plans fully funded. However, due to the long-lasting impact of the pandemic and limited capacity in strategic planning, many national statistical offices are implementing expired strategic plans that may not meet emerging data needs.

Status of implementation of statistical plans, 2022, (number of countries and territories)

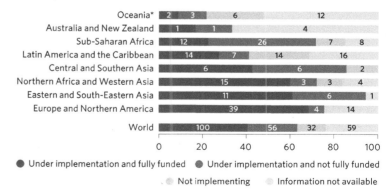

● Under implementation and fully funded   ● Under implementation and not fully funded
● Not implementing   ● Information not available

* Excluding Australia and New Zealand.

---

4   Since 2018, the OECD has been publishing data on headline ODA volume and ODA as proportion of GNI on the grant equivalent basis. SDG 17.2.1 is measured on a net ODA basis; therefore, the figures presented here may differ slightly.

III. Breaking through to a better future for all

The sobering picture of the Sustainable Development Goals being in reverse halfway to our 2030 deadline is a clarion call to the world to redouble our efforts to eliminate poverty and hunger, advance gender equality and overcome the triple planetary crisis of climate change, nature and biodiversity loss and pollution. Failure to heed that call will fuel greater political instability and displacement, further erode trust in public institutions, upend economies and lead to irreversible existential changes to our natural environment. Above all, it will cause immense suffering for current and future generations – especially among the world's poorest and most vulnerable people and countries.

But we can turn things around. Although the overall picture is deeply concerning, the data also offers a glimpse of the possible, showing progress in a number of key areas from energy to Internet access and more. There is also ample evidence that the transformation demanded by the Goals is one of immense opportunity. And in the years since 2015, we have seen Governments, the private sector and the general public embracing the Sustainable Development Goals.

The Goals remain a truly inspiring and unifying compass, and transformative progress can be made even in the face of adversity. Furthermore, this generation is equipped with knowledge, technologies and resources unprecedented in history and can draw on a wide range of normative frameworks. Breaking through to a better future for all demands that we put this advantage to use to lift hundreds of millions of people out of poverty, advance gender equality, put our world on a low-emissions pathway by 2030 and secure human rights for all.

The 2023 Global Sustainable Development Report provides a synopsis of evidence showing that we can guide transformation toward sustainable and equitable outcomes. The sections below complement its findings and provide Member States with analysis and recommendations to unlock the rapid and deep transitions needed to deliver the Goals by 2030. The United Nations system will seek to mobilize support for a number of them, through a set of high impact initiatives in the lead-up to and following the SDG Summit.

World leaders should come together at the SDG Summit to deliver a rescue plan for people and planet centred around the following three major breakthroughs:

Equipping governance and institutions for sustainable and inclusive transformation

Prioritizing policies and investments that have multiplier effects across the goals

Securing a surge in Sustainable Development Goals financing and an enabling global environment for developing countries

A. Equipping governance and institutions for sustainable and inclusive transformation

Delivering change at the speed and scale required by the Sustainable Development Goals demands more than ever before from public institutions and political leaders. It requires bold decisions, the transfer of resources from one sector to another, the creation of a new regulatory environment, the appropriate deployment of new technologies, the advancement of longer-term holistic perspectives, the mobilizing of a wide range of actors and the capacity to advance disruptive change while strengthening trust and social cohesion.[1] Each of those dimensions presents challenges for political leadership and public governance systems. Together, they constitute a set of demands for which contemporary governance systems were not built. It is essential therefore to take action to equip governance systems for transformation.

Since 2015, Governments have responded to the Sustainable Development Goals in a variety of ways. Yet voluntary national reviews and research studies demonstrate that nationalization of the Goals has not yet had the necessary "normative and institutional impact, from legislative action to changing resource allocation".[2] The Goals must become more than a means to communicate change. They must become a guiding star that shapes national policies, budgets, institutions and long-term national development planning.

They must become the core business of presidents and prime ministers, of parliaments and the private sector.

Incentivizing, steering and advancing transformation is complex and can often result in unintended consequences or trade-offs. Public institutions and public servants need to have capacities and strategies to continually revisit and adjust policy implementation in order to maximize benefits and capitalize on synergies while understanding trade-offs and identifying feedback loops, including by leveraging international human rights and labour standards. They also need to be able to work across sectors and contribute, including with budget alignment, to a whole-of-government approach to the Goals. The ability of institutions to steer and leverage digital technologies, in an inclusive and equitable manner, is also essential, as is a capacity to work in unison with the private sector and others to advance the public interest.

Localization, anchored on the principle of multilevel governance and multistakeholder collaboration, is a key approach to collectively propel us towards greater inclusion and sustainability. Local and regional governments have a key role to play in this process since 65 per cent of the Sustainable

---

[1] See www.idlo.int/system/files/event-documents/2021_sdg16_conference_report_05072021.pdf.
[2] See www.nature.com/articles/s41893-022-00909-5.

Development Goals targets are linked to their work and mandates. As the sphere of government closest to local communities, they are essential for responding to the erosion of the social contract and for protecting our societies amid intersecting global crises. Since 2018, the voluntary local review global movement has provided an unprecedented push towards localization. The more than 200 voluntary local reviews carried out to date have shed light on and raised the profile of local action as part of national action and international processes. In addition, the reviews have contributed to advances in all dimensions of localization of the Goals – from data innovation to planning and policy coherence, and to project development and financing. Even so, the resources of local and regional governments – financial, human and technical – remain limited across the globe, hindering their capacities to deliver basic services and drive development at the local level.

The private sector is a critical driver of productivity, employment and growth. Business leaders are increasingly acknowledging the necessity and urgency of taking sustainability factors into account to achieve long-term success. Businesses are making sustainability and climate-related commitments daily. They must be held accountable for those commitments, and they must deliver. Corporate governance models, incentive structures and operating practices must be adjusted to align with the objectives of sustainable development. Policies and regulations must facilitate long-term decision-making, include the pricing of externalities and phase out harmful subsidies. And we must see an improvement in the transparency and credibility of sustainability labels and ratings, ensuring that all efforts are made to eliminate rampant green-washing and Goals-washing.

Culture is a global public good and a critical enabler and driver of progress towards the Goals. Culture serves as a source of knowledge, values and communication, as a contributor to environmental sustainability and as a generator of economic activity and jobs. Respect for cultural diversity

and the diversity of religions and beliefs, as well as intercultural dialogue and understanding, are also crucial for strengthening social cohesion and sustaining peace. Culture and respect for cultural diversity, however, remain undervalued and underutilized in the push for Goals-related progress. Greater consideration of culture's role in supporting the achievement of the Goals – including within relevant indicators – would generate an important boost for implementation of the Goals between now and 2030.

Access to timely and high-quality disaggregated data is essential. It can multiply the efficiency and effectiveness of domestic and development spending, generating a "data dividend" for implementation of the Goals. Yet many countries lack the resources and capacities necessary to respond to data demands and, as highlighted in section II above, there remain significant gaps in the geographic coverage, timeliness and disaggregation of Goals indicators. Domestic spending on data and statistics is low, and some 40 per cent of national statistics offices saw a drop in funding during the pandemic. There is little transparency around donor support in this area, and one study estimated that development cooperation spending on data had dropped by more than 20 per cent between 2018 and 2020. Greater use of new data sources and innovative approaches – including geospatial information, remote sensing, artificial intelligence and machine learning, crowd sourcing, qualitative methods, citizen-generated data and private sector data – represent new opportunities, although they are not without their own risks and challenges. Strong data governance, data literacy and data protection policies are essential, but today only about half of the least developed countries have such laws.[3] Much more can be done to strengthen data ecosystems, and support from the United Nations and other international partners must also become more cohesive and effective.

Effective engagement with the global public and effective follow-up to Sustainable Development Goals commitments and implementation efforts are essential to understanding progress, boosting public ownership and identifying major objectives. By July 2023, 188 countries will have conducted voluntary national reviews – the central instrument for Goals-related follow-up and review at the global and national levels. Overall, countries have improved the preparation of their reviews, engaging stakeholders more systematically and combining multiple tools of analysis. Voluntary national reviews have also had a spill-over effect at the subnational level, with the growth of voluntary local reviews as a key example. With the Goals so far off track, and building on the lessons learned since 2015, it is time to take Goals-related follow-up to the next level. It is essential for our attention to shift from reporting national action to an international audience to strengthening national accountability for progress and transformation. This calls for a systematic inclusion of Goals-related implementation efforts in national oversight systems, for more independent evaluations of national implementation, for the greater involvement of scientists in monitoring and review, and for a fundamental rethink of the voluntary national review process.

Priority actions

 Call upon all countries to deliver a national commitment to transformation of the Goals at the SDG Summit, including by setting national benchmarks for reducing poverty and inequality, making achievement of the Goals a central focus in national planning and oversight mechanisms, and aligning national and subnational budgets with the Goals.

 Invest in public sector capacity and infrastructure to identify trade-offs and drive large-scale change, enable complex decision-making, leverage digital technologies and boost implementation partnerships.

---

3   See https://unctad.org/page/data-protection-and-privacy-legislation-worldwide.

Recognize the central role of local and subnational governments in implementing the Goals, including by designing national enabling frameworks to allow subnational governments to meet their devolved responsibilities and by strengthening their capacities and resources to advance the Goals. Crisis mitigation, adaptation, preparedness and recovery, should be anchored on the principles of multilevel governance, and multistakeholder and multisectoral collaboration.

Encourage the development of effective policies and a suitable regulatory framework to support the alignment of private sector governance models, operating practices and disclosure requirements with sustainable development objectives.

Give due consideration to the contribution of culture to the achievement of sustainable development in the formulation of national, regional and international development policies and international cooperation instruments.

Take action to reap the data dividend, with a focus on the most vulnerable groups, by working towards securing data for at least 90 per cent of the Sustainable Development Goals targets in each country by 2027, increasing domestic financing for data and statistics by 50 per cent from current levels by 2030, embracing new data sources and innovative approaches, and adopting data governance and protection policies. Donors should also commit to increasing the share of ODA for data to at least 0.7 per cent by 2030, for the full implementation of the Cape Town Global Action Plan for Sustainable Development Data.

Take monitoring, follow-up and review of the Sustainable Development Goals to the next level by boosting independent evaluations of implementation, strengthening engagement with parliament and civil society, centring voluntary national reviews on national commitments to transformation of the Goals, establishing official registration systems of voluntary local reviews and supporting the further development of Goals indicators with disaggregated data.

B. Prioritizing policies and investments that will drive just transitions and unlock progress across the goals

1. Close divides to leave no one behind

Recent crises have exposed unequal coping mechanisms and deepened divides across various dimensions of well-being. As shown in section II of the present report, above, the decades-long trend of narrowing global income inequality has reversed, more people are fleeing conflict than at any time on record, and the slum population is growing. The impacts of those reversals are felt most by women and girls and by vulnerable and marginalized populations, including persons with disabilities, migrants, refugees and internally displaced persons, and Indigenous Peoples.

The world must act to close gaps and improve the well-being of the people farthest behind and thus contribute to stability and resilience globally. Action in the areas below can also have multiplier impacts across the Sustainable Development Goals.

In 2015, the Sustainable Development Goals were agreed as an integrated and indivisible set of Goals and they cannot be achieved one at a time or in siloes. In the 2019 and 2023 editions of the Global Sustainable Development Report, the evidence-based case is made that transformation towards sustainable development will be possible only if actions address systems of goals and targets. Policy actions are needed to drive key transitions and to serve as multipliers that advance progress across the Goals. National priorities and contexts will determine the precise mix of policies and interventions, but combining actions and actors geared to leave no one behind with those that balance human well-being and the stewardship of nature can help build a holistic approach.

Provide shock-responsive, adaptive and universal social protection, and strengthen action to generate jobs for a just transition

Social protection and jobs creation and retention are the only refuge for the large segments of society with no financial buffers and are crucial tools for reducing and preventing poverty, in particular when crises hit. During the pandemic, many Governments rapidly expanded social protection coverage or benefits, often with digital tools, but many were one-time payments or short-term solutions.[4] Most of those additional social protection and job retention measures were implemented in advanced economies with the resources to do so. In developing countries, many Governments now face the prospect of having to roll back those measures in response to compounding fiscal pressures.

---

4   Maya Hammad, Fabianna Bacil and Fábio Veras Soares, Next Practices – *Innovations in the COVID-19 social protection responses and beyond* (UNDP, 2021), available from https://socialprotection.org/discover/publications/next-practices-innovations-covid-19-social-protection-responses-and-beyond.

In addition, social protection coverage often excludes those who need it the most, such as informal workers, in particular women.[5] For instance, only 28 per cent of persons with significant disabilities have access to disability benefits globally, and only 1 per cent in low-income countries.[6] The current global economic slowdown is also likely to force more workers to accept lower quality and poorly paid jobs that lack job security and social protection. The need for universal social protection and decent job opportunities will only grow as the transitions to green and digital economic systems accelerate and as demographic transitions unfold.

Despite the devastating impact of today's cascading crises on social protection and livelihood opportunities, these shocks have also highlighted the opportunities for driving progress. Right now, there is a window of opportunity to cement some of the gains and learn from positive experiences, with impacts that can cut across the Sustainable Development Goals.[7] Social protection that is dynamic in terms of both coverage and the means of distribution can bolster capabilities to weather crises. There is also a strong investment case for expanding social protection and supporting job creation: investing in the care economy, for example, could generate 280 million jobs globally, while investing in the green and circular economy could create 100 million jobs, both by 2030. The revenue from this job creation could fuel a virtuous cycle that can accelerate just transitions and create more resilient, inclusive and equitable societies for all. Despite high up-front costs in some cases, investing in these areas will yield long-term results that far outweigh immediate costs. Despite high interest rates, inflation and fragile debt situations, long-term, affordable financing to support social protection and decent job creation opportunities can and must be found. The United Nations Global Accelerator on Jobs and Social Protection for Just Transitions, launched in September 2021, is supporting the design and implementation of inclusive and integrated policies and investment strategies for decent jobs with social protection, to support just transitions for all. It also aims to establish national financing frameworks and mobilize public and private domestic and international resources, with the aim of expanding social protection to 4 billion people and creating 400 million new, decent jobs by 2030.

Priority actions

Expand investments in social protection floors as a percentage of GDP in national budgets and make institutional changes to promote an integrated approach to achieving adaptive, shock-responsive and universal social protection and creating new, decent job opportunities in the care, digital and green economies.

Mobilize political efforts through the United Nations Global Accelerator on Jobs and Social Protection for Just Transitions to channel funds from international, national, public and private sources, including from the international financial institutions, towards this aim.

Create active labour market policies to help workers upskill and re-skill in order to keep or change their job, adapt to the green and digital transitions and find ways out of poverty.

Fully leverage digital technology to expand the foundations – including registries, digital IDs and financial inclusion – on which more comprehensive, dynamic and adaptive social protection systems can be built.

Invest in women and girls

Current rates of progress towards gender equality are set to leave half of the world's population and the world's workforce behind. Gender parity for labour-force participation had been slowing since 2009 – and it reversed in 2020.[8] Women make about half as much as men do and carry a disproportionate share of care work, both paid and unpaid, which increased during the pandemic.[9] Rates of violence against women were reported to have increased considerably during the pandemic. By one measure, GDP per capita would be almost 20 per cent higher if all gender employment gaps were closed.[10] This demands a dismantling of discriminatory laws, a shake-up in the existing social structures and norms, and the use of special measures and quotas for the targeted investment in women.

The world's population is also drastically changing. According to a recent United Nations study, greater parity in the labour force would do more to sustain economies in ageing, low-fertility societies than setting targets for women to have more children. Yet it is estimated that, globally, the number of unintended pregnancies every year is a staggering 121 million, or an average of 331,000 per day. Safeguarding access to quality sexual and reproductive health for all and instituting family-friendly policies are the best ways to ensure that people can achieve their individual reproductive goals and optimize their contribution to society.

Priority actions

Leverage special measures and quotas to promote gender parity across all levels of decision-making in political and economic life; and accelerate women's economic inclusion by closing the digital divide, investing in women-owned businesses and reducing the unpaid care and domestic burden for women and girls.

Dismantle all discriminatory laws and practices, take action to shape social norms that promote gender equality and ensure universal access to sexual and reproductive health and reproductive rights.

Pass laws and put in place emergency response plans that prevent and eliminate violence against women and girls, both online and offline, by 2025.

Make the digital transformation work for everyone

Persistent digital divides among and within countries stand in the way of widespread Goals-related progress and hamper the use of new data

5   See www.wiego.org/resources/long-economic-covid-worlds-working-class-infographic.
6   United Nations, "Policy brief: a disability-inclusive response to COVID-19" (May 2020), available at https://unsdg.un.org/sites/default/files/2020-05/Policy-Brief-A-Disability-Inclusive-Response-to-COVID-19.pdf.
7   International Labour Organization, Food and Agriculture Organization of the United Nations and United Nations Children's Fund (UNICEF), UN collaboration on social protection: Reaching consensus on how to accelerate social protection systems-building (Geneva, 2022), available from https://socialprotection.org/discover/publications/un-collaboration-social-protection-reaching-consensus-how-accelerate-social.
8   World Economic Forum, Global Gender Gap Report 2022 (Geneva, 2022), available from www.weforum.org/reports/global-gender-gap-report-2022/.
9   OECD, "Caregiving in Crisis: Gender inequality in paid and unpaid work during COVID-19" (2021), available at www.oecd.org/coronavirus/policy-responses/caregiving-in-crisis-gender-inequality-in-paid-and-unpaid-work-during-covid-19-3555d164/.
10 See https://openknowledge.worldbank.org/handle/10986/37062.

sources. These gaps should be tackled holistically, not just at a whole-of-government level but also at a whole-of-system level, with a focus on infrastructure, digital skills and inclusive environments, supported by the global development community.

Navigating the double-edged sword of digital transformation, managing digital risks and digital harms and leveraging the potential of technologies, requires investing in inclusive and accessible digital infrastructure to ensure meaningful connectivity for all. The large gaps in access to technologies, connectivity and infrastructure – as well as the poor accessibility of technologies themselves for groups such as persons with disabilities – have significant human rights and development implications. For instance, only one person in 10 in the world has access to assistive technology products and services.[11] The proliferation of robotics, artificial intelligence, quantum computing, the Internet of things and cloud and mobile computing can support human well-being and the Sustainable Development Goals. Enhancing digital literacy and data literacy in and outside the public sector should focus on self-reliance and lifelong learning. Effective digital partnerships with the private sector and other stakeholders can produce applications to advance progress towards the Goals. The development by Member States of a global digital compact is under way and would be a step in the direction of making digital technologies work for the public good.

Priority actions

 Invest in foundational inclusive and accessible digital infrastructures to ensure meaningful connectivity for all and build digital literacy and data literacy in and outside the public sector.

 Incentivize digital partnerships with the private sector and other stakeholders to produce applications that further Goals-related progress.

Adopt a life-course approach to essential services and urgently tackle the global crisis in education

Early and consistent investments in access to essential social services and social inclusion can improve the prospects for work and well-being later in life and are fundamental to a strong social contract. Interventions during early childhood and adolescence can prevent subsequent limitations and support socioeconomic mobility, while interventions in adulthood or older age can help individuals recover from past deprivations. However, systems today continue to take a fragmented approach. The limited focus on a life-course and intergenerational approach and inadequate access to training opportunities for older persons hamper their ability to continue working or find new employment.

Quality inclusive education is key to preparing today's young people for high-skill jobs and is a major contributor to health and well-being, gender equality and climate mitigation.[12] However, against the backdrop of pandemic-related lost learning, education today is in deep crisis. In low- and middle-income countries, the share of children living in learning poverty – unable to read and understand a simple statement about everyday life at age 10 - could possibly

reach 70 per cent,[13] with children with disabilities and other marginalized groups suffering disproportionately. As highlighted at the 2022 Transforming Education Summit, ending the current crisis and making education fit to tackle the world's most pressing issues demands a sea-change in how Governments and the international community approach and invest in education. Recent analysis shows that almost $100 billion a year is needed to allow countries to meet their national benchmarks for achieving Goal 4. A forthcoming policy brief on transforming education will elaborate on this challenge as an input to the preparations for the Summit of the Future. The crisis in education is, however, a ticking time bomb. Urgent and focused action now will reap benefits for generations to come.

Priority actions

 Expand access to early childhood education, nutrition and health care, and leverage the forthcoming high-level meeting on universal health coverage to strengthen national health systems.

 Equip social protection systems to address needs that arise naturally during the life cycle and during periods of low earning capacity, such as childhood, disability, childbearing and old age.

 Deliver on national statements of commitment to transform education by taking concrete steps to invest more, more equitably and more efficiently in education, monitoring progress at all levels and taking corrective action to improve basic literacy, numeracy and digital literacy proficiency, ensuring a future-oriented focus in education curricula and pedagogy and leveraging technologies for greater access and learning.

Invest in peace

The data in section II of the present report show that one quarter of humanity lives in a conflict-affected area. Development cannot wait in these areas. Investments in peace and sustainable development generate a virtuous cycle – with development gains addressing the drivers of conflict and inclusive peace enabling development priorities to expand.

Advancing the Sustainable Development Goals in conflict affected regions and those with humanitarian needs will break cycles of dependency and address the underlying drivers of vulnerability. It is vital to ensure that persons affected by instability, conflict or violence have access to services and protection, including the more than 100 million forcibly displaced people worldwide, of whom more than 32 million are refugees.[14] Countries affected by conflict or humanitarian disaster need their partners and supporters to act coherently. They need peacebuilders, development practitioners and humanitarians who can see the bigger picture. They need partners who do not work in isolation. The United Nations must lead by example. All United Nations entities should work coherently and simultaneously to advance development priorities, meet humanitarian needs and build peace.

The New Agenda for Peace, being prepared for the Summit of the Future, will seek to reduce strategic risks by strengthening international foresight and capacities to identify and adapt to new risks and to focus on preventing conflict.[15]

---

11 See www.who.int/health-topics/assistive-technology#tab=tab_2.
12 Cordero EC, Centeno D, Todd AM (2020) The role of climate change education on individual lifetime carbon emissions. PLoS ONE 15(2): e0206266. https://doi.org/10.1371/journal.pone.0206266.
13 United Nations Educational, Scientific and Cultural Organization (UNESCO), UNICEF and World Bank, *The State of the Global Education Crisis: A Path to Recovery* (Washington, D.C., Paris and New York, 2021), available from https://documents1.worldbank.org/curated/en/416991638768297704/pdf/The-State-of-the-Global-Education-Crisis-A-Path-to-Recovery.pdf.
14 See www.unhcr.org/refugee-statistics/.
15 See https://dppa.un.org/en/new-agenda-for-peace.

Strengthen investment in development priorities in conflict-affected areas and areas with humanitarian needs to address the underlying drivers of vulnerability.

Proactively integrate persons and communities affected by instability, conflict or violence, especially refugees and internally displaced persons, into national systems of health care, education and employment.

2. Leverage environment-human well-being synergies

Human well-being is integrally connected to the stewardship of nature and protection of the environment – the air, water, land and ecosystems that are foundations for life. Achieving the 2030 Agenda for Sustainable Development and the Paris Agreement depends on safeguarding these resources for sustainability, equality and justice. If the current trajectory towards climate change, biodiversity loss, pollution and the degradation of ecosystems goes unaddressed, progress on the Sustainable Development Goals could unravel, exacerbating hunger, poverty, conflict, natural disasters and public health emergencies. However, acting now in the below areas could boost progress across the Goals and support the promise to leave no one behind.

Accelerate access to energy for all and the shift to renewables

Access to electricity in developing countries has increased, even during the current period of crisis, while a lack of access to clean cooking solutions remains stubbornly persistent. The pace of progress needs to accelerate, along with the reliability and affordability to reach everyone. This needs to happen while also ensuring the transition to renewable energy systems, supported by measures to increase energy efficiency.

Immediate, deep, rapid and sustained reductions in the greenhouse gas emissions of the energy sector is imperative in order to preserve the 1.5°C goal of the Paris Agreement, since energy accounts for more than two thirds of global greenhouse gas emissions.[16] Accelerating the renewables revolution is our best hope of ensuring energy security, affordability, access and independence, while keeping the 1.5°C target alive. At the same time, the transition to renewables must be proactively managed to minimize social disruption and maximize the many socioeconomic benefits, including economic growth, poverty eradication and job creation during the transition. Using solar and wind power to replace coal could save $23 billion a year.[17] The transition would create 24 million to 25 million new jobs, far more than the 6 million to 7 million jobs that will be lost.[18]

Priority actions

Take immediate action to advance the global transition from fossil fuels to renewable energy, as proposed in my climate Acceleration Agenda:

• No new coal-fired power plants and their phase-out by 2030 in OECD countries by and 2040 in all other countries; end all international public and private funding of coal;

• Ensure net-zero electricity generation by 2035 for all developed economies and by 2040 for the rest of the world;

• Cease all licensing or funding of new oil and gas reserves – consistent with the findings of the International Energy Agency; stop any expansion of existing oil and gas reserves;

• Support the preparation of investment-ready energy transition plans consistent with these actions.

Address critical bottlenecks to the deployment of renewables in developing countries by ensuring access to battery storage technology, fostering resilient and diversified supply chains for critical raw materials, and by tackling the high cost of capital for renewables in the developing world.

Triple finance and investment for renewable energy and energy efficiency, including by shifting fossil fuel subsidies to renewables and reforming the international financial architecture.

Mobilizing financing to support energy compacts; call upon multilateral development banks, development finance institutions and bilateral agencies to do their part by taking more risk and developing or repurposing financial instruments to lower the cost of capital for renewable technologies – this can help expand cooperative models for the renewable energy transition, such as the Just Energy Transition Partnerships.

Strengthen international cooperation and collaboration to ensure transparency, accountability and credibility for these actions.

Secure food, water and sanitation systems

Business-as-usual approaches are neither protecting the right to food and water for a growing population nor safeguarding the environment to sustain and secure the provision of these resources. Efforts to address hunger and food security are falling behind, even as direct greenhouse gas emissions from agriculture are projected to increase by 6 per cent during the next decade.[19] Furthermore, access to clean water and water management are at risk as climate disasters increase and several regions face severe water scarcity. Low access to sanitation and hygiene remains a major and urgent challenge with devastating impacts on health, human dignity and the situation of women and girls. Rapid urbanization intensifies these challenges but also offers opportunities to build more resilient, cost-efficient and inclusive cities. The nexus of food, water, sanitation and environment sustainability must factor into development pathways holistically and coherently, with adequate human, technological and financial resources.

Since the 2021 Food Systems Summit, 117 countries have developed national food system transformation pathways – with some having started implementing their pathways while others need technical and financial

---

16 See www.iea.org/data-and-statistics/data-tools/greenhouse-gas-emissions-from-energy-data-explorer.

17 International Renewable Energy Agency, *Renewable Power Generation Costs in 2019* (Abu Dhabi, 2019), available from www.irena.org/publications/2020/Jun/Renewable-Power-Costs-in-2019.

18 ILO, *World Employment and Social Outlook 2018: Greening with jobs* (Geneva, 2018), available from www.ilo.org/global/publications/books/WCMS_628654/lang--en/index.htm.

19 See www.oecd-ilibrary.org/docserver/f1b0b29cen.pdf?expires=1678719176&id=id&accname=guest&checksum=D46813AB4B74489CA8839EE6843A7CF3.

assistance to move forward. System complexities are being built into emerging initiatives using data from socioeconomic models and biophysical models. The United Nations Water Conference, held in March 2023, mobilized new commitments to solve the water and sanitation crisis, with the potential to generate dividends across the Sustainable Development Goals. For every dollar invested in water and sanitation, there is a $4.30 return in reduced health-care costs for individuals and society.[20]

Priority actions

 Integrate decision-making in the water, energy, food and environment sectors to ensure good nutrition, strengthen food and water security and sanitation, support climate action and maintain biodiversity and forests.

 Advance national pathways developed after the 2021 Food Systems Summit and on commitments at the 2023 United Nations Water Conference, engaging all sectors and stakeholders.

 Coordinate policy efforts across countries to better meet nutritional needs while addressing climate change and inefficient water and land use.

 Invest in green infrastructure to upgrade ageing infrastructure for water management to ensure water access and reduce pollution.

Protect biodiversity and natural resources

The environmental resources that sustain life are under threat, with trends moving backward since the adoption of the 2030 Agenda. Yet more than half of the world's GDP is highly or moderately dependent on nature.[21] Some 1.6 billion people's livelihoods depend on forests, where the highest levels of terrestrial biodiversity are found, making sustainable land management critical to human well-being and poverty reduction. Another 680 million people live in coastal megacities. Many coastal dwellers rely on aquaculture for their livelihoods, and nearly half the world's people depend on fish for protein. Striking a better balance with nature is also a health priority. Land degradation and habitat fragmentation drive humans and wildlife into closer contact, reducing biodiversity and increasing the risk of future pandemics through the spread of zoonotic disease.

Protecting nature is also crucial for climate action, as forests and oceans help mitigate climate change by absorbing carbon dioxide. Oceans absorb one third of carbon emissions released into the atmosphere, but increased absorption of carbon dioxide leads to ocean warming and acidification, ice-melting, sea-level rise and marine heatwaves, threatening the natural marine ecosystems and populations reliant on oceans for their lives and livelihoods.

The recent adoption of the Kunming-Montreal Global Biodiversity Framework at the culmination of the 15th United Nations Biodiversity Conference represents a landmark agreement by Governments to guide actions and funding to safeguard nature, protect indigenous rights and sustainably manage other critical resources by 2030. The 2018 Regional Agreement on Access to Information, Public Participation and Access to Justice in Environmental Matters in Latin America and the Caribbean can facilitate implementation of global sustainable development agreements.

Priority actions

 Strengthen links between public health and the conservation and sustainable use of biodiversity in sectoral policies.

 Raise government and stakeholder awareness, as well as capacity for monitoring and predicting the impacts of biodiversity loss on human well-being.

 Follow up on the goals and targets of the Kunming-Montreal Global Biodiversity Framework; and close the $700 billion biodiversity finance gap. Increase financing from all sources by at least $500 billion per year, and eliminate and reform incentives harmful to biodiversity.

Prevent new and reduce existing disaster risks

COVID-19, conflict and climate disasters have shown just how vulnerable Goals-related progress can be to shocks. Systematically integrating risk considerations into planning for the 2030 Agenda can reduce the consequences of shocks, especially for the vulnerable, and the likelihood of crises. It is also important to acknowledge that actions in one system can create or reduce risks for another, as hazards cascade across systems.

Countries can shock-proof Goals-related progress by strengthening risk management governance and adopting a multi-hazard and multisectoral approach to dealing with pandemics or climate change that can disrupt societal and economic networks. The integration of disaster risk reduction with climate, sustainable development and humanitarian action is also needed, shifting the balance from responding to investing. The United Nations policy brief on an emergency platform to strengthen the international response to complex global shocks, an input into the preparations for the Summit of the Future, outlines how a more predictable and structured response can help mitigate the risks to the most vulnerable countries.

Strengthening disaster risk resilience requires leadership at the highest level of government, engagement from all sectors and multistakeholder participation. My initiative to ensure universal coverage of multi-hazard early warning systems can ensure minimal loss of lives and livelihoods when disasters strike. Collaborating to develop new tracking systems to record and analyse hazardous events and disaster losses and damages can also help. Greater investments in capacity-building and transformative action on investments to accelerate Goals-related progress pave the way for greater strategic foresight and the implementation of national disaster risk reduction financing.

Priority actions

 Systematically integrate risk considerations into planning for the 2030 Agenda by fully implementing the Sendai Framework for Disaster Risk Reduction 2015–2030.

 Ensure universal coverage of multi-hazard early warning systems by 2027.

 Link global data for public health emergencies and other disasters.

---

20 See https://news.un.org/en/story/2014/11/484032#:~:text=For%20every%20dollar%20invested%20in,United%20Nat ions%20World%20Health%20Organization.
21 Intergovernmental Science-Policy Platform on Biodiversity and Ecosystem Services, *Global assessment report of the Intergovernmental Science-Policy Platform on Biodiversity and Ecosystem Services* (Bonn, Germany, 2019), available from www.ipbes.net/global-assessment.

Rising inflation, unsustainable debt burdens, the COVID-19 pandemic, and the impacts of the war in Ukraine on the costs of food and energy and financing have significantly reduced countries' fiscal space, undermining their ability to invest in recovery efforts. Despite increased support from the international community to developing countries, these efforts have remained inadequate, exacerbated by an international financial system that is not fit for purpose and that remains plagued with systemic and historic inequities.

In addition, developing countries struggle to gain equitable access to the global trading system and to the benefits of new technologies and the fruits of science and innovation – all of which continue to favour those countries that have benefitted historically from protectionism and global resource extraction.

To reverse course and turbocharge the Sustainable Development Goals, it is essential for countries to have the resources they need at scale to invest in both their immediate recovery and in long-term sustainable development outcomes, including climate action. This requires a two-pronged approach that aims to secure a surge in Goals-related financing, while simultaneously reforming the international financial architecture to make it resilient, equitable and accessible for all. It is also critical that developing countries have better access to global trade, science, technology and innovation.

Deliver a Sustainable Development Goals stimulus and reform the international financial architecture

To secure a surge in Goals-related financing in the short term, the Sustainable Development Goals stimulus plan calls for an additional $500 billion per year in financing for sustainable development, to be delivered through mutually reinforcing concessional and non-concessional finance.

The Sustainable Development Goals stimulus puts forward three main areas for immediate action: (a) tackle the high cost of debt and rising risks of debt distress, including by converting short-term, high interest borrowing into long-term (more than 30-year) debt at lower interest rates; (b) massively scale-up affordable long-term financing for development, especially through multilateral development banks and by aligning all financing flows with the

Goals; and (c) expand contingency financing to all countries in need. The Sustainable Development Goals stimulus also aims to ensure that resources are invested in the areas needed to secure the Goals and just transitions. Countries should align all forms of finance with the Goals, using tools such as Goals-aligned integrated national financing frameworks.

Urgent action is also needed to prevent tax evasion and avoidance and illicit financial flows, to boost international tax cooperation and to strengthen national fiscal capacities for domestic resource mobilization.[22] All countries can use globally agreed concepts and tested methods to curb illicit finance. Making budgets more credible and increasing the efficiency of budget execution are also critical.

While the Sustainable Development Goals stimulus can be achieved within the confines of the current financial architecture, adequate long-term financing requires the reform of the international financial architecture in order to overcome the major structural barriers that predominantly serve wealthy countries and individuals. This calls for delivering on the Addis Ababa Action Agenda and other international frameworks. It also calls for ambitious efforts in order to: (a) go beyond GDP when determining access to concessional finance; (b) create new financing models for global public goods; (c) change the business models of multilateral development banks, aligning their mandates and operational models with the Goals; (d) strengthen the global financial safety net; (e) improve debt ratings; and (f) create an effective sovereign debt workout mechanism. And it calls for reforming the international financial architecture and global economic governance structures to make them more inclusive and representative. These and other areas will be elaborated in forthcoming policy briefs on reforming the international financial architecture and developing metrics beyond GDP, which will be part of a series of crucial inputs to Member States as part of preparations for the 2024 Summit of the Future. The International Conference on Financing for Development in 2025 will provide a clear pathway to secure progress on the full range of issues addressed in the Addis Ababa Action Agenda.

International and domestic private investment in emerging and developing economies must be scaled up. The Global Investors for Sustainable Development Alliance has put forward a definition of sustainable development investing to guide the private sector. It calls for sustainable development investing in ways that contribute to sustainable development, using the Sustainable Development Goals as a basis for measurement. Attracting such investment at scale requires strong institutions and a conducive regulatory and operating environment. Transparent de-risking mechanisms and guarantees around key risk markers must be scaled up to secure greater private investment in the Goals without saddling Governments with even more debt.

Priority actions

 Urge all countries and financial institutions to deliver the Sustainable Development Goals stimulus and massively scale up financing for the Goals to at least $500 billion per year.

 Reform of the international financial architecture, and encourage tangible progress on reform of multilateral development banks, increasing their capitalization, supporting the re-channelling

---

[22] https://factipanel.org/docpdfs/FACTI_Report_ExecSum.pdf.

of special drawing rights through multilateral development banks, better leveraging their capital bases, securing increases to grants and concessional finance, and increasing their risk appetites. Also essential is providing de-risking mechanisms and guarantees to attract private finance, and reforming their business practices by explicitly linking their mandates to the Goals, including climate action.

 Encourage the development of fair and effective tax systems, aligned internationally, to support financing efforts at the national level, including through Goals-aligned integrated national financing frameworks.

 Decide to convene the Fourth International Conference on Financing for Development in 2025, building on the 2024 Summit of the Future and the proposed United Nations Biennial Summit with the members of the Group of 20 and the members of the Economic and Social Council, as well as heads of international financial institutions.

Harness trade to work for the Sustainable Development Goals

Trade is a critical driver of economic growth, job creation and poverty reduction in developed and developing countries alike. But to realize the benefits, developing countries must overcome various barriers and challenges that prevent their integration in regional and global value chains and investment networks.

One major obstacle to trade is high transport costs, which can make goods uncompetitive in global markets. Developing countries also face price fluctuations for primary commodities, which can lead to volatile and unpredictable export earnings. Unpredictable supply chains hinder the timely delivery of intermediary and final goods, a problem clearly illustrated during the COVID-19 pandemic. Cumbersome customs processes and protectionist policies further impede trade flows. Moreover, the shift towards knowledge-intensive services – such as professional services, government services, information technology services and telecommunications – has highlighted the importance of digital infrastructure and literacy. Data flows, which have been growing at close to 50 per cent annually between 2010 and 2019, make digital infrastructure fundamental.

Despite those challenges, several recent developments have generated new momentum for leveraging trade for the Sustainable Development Goals. The COVID-19 pandemic prompted emergency policies to remove trade and financial roadblocks to accelerate the delivery of vaccines, therapeutics and diagnostics. The Initiative on the Safe Transportation of Grain and Foodstuffs from Ukrainian Ports has helped countries to withstand shocks to trade caused by the war in Ukraine. The African Trade Exchange Platform is helping to address food, fuel and fertilizer shortages in developing countries. After more than two decades of negotiations, WTO members reached the landmark and novel multilateral Agreement on Fisheries Subsidies. The global system of trade preferences among developing countries is only one ratification away from entry into force – a move that would allow preferential tariff treatment, generating shared welfare gains of $14 billion.

To maximize the role of trade in achieving the Sustainable Development Goals, it is crucial to strengthen the multilateral trading system and align it with the Goals. This system should be universal, rules-based, open, non-discriminatory and equitable. At the same time, developing countries need support to build productive capacity and infrastructure to connect

with regional and global production and supply chains, by meeting environmental requirements and using digital trade infrastructures for e-commerce. Approaches should be inclusive of micro, small and medium-sized enterprises, and women-owned enterprises, with progress measured by sex-disaggregated trade and business statistics. Developing countries also need the policy space to implement coherent industrial, innovation, trade and investment policies to mainstream trade into national and sector strategies in support of the Goals. Collaboration at the multilateral level is also essential to address vulnerabilities in supply, transport, distribution chain infrastructure, and trade finance for micro-, small and medium-sized enterprises to reduce disruptions from climate change, conflict and future pandemics.

Priority actions:

 Strengthen a universal, rules-based, open, non-discriminatory and equitable multilateral trading system, and call for the alignment of trade regimes and national complementary policies with the Goals.

 Provide support to developing countries, including by scaling up aid for trade, to build productive capacity, connect with regional and global production and supply chains and boost trade in goods and services that contribute to the energy transition and decarbonization of supply chains.

 Ensure open, fair and contestable markets through competition and consumer policies, and collaborate at the multilateral level to address vulnerabilities in supply, transport and distribution chain infrastructure to increase resilience to conflict, future pandemics and climate change.

Revolutionize science, technology and innovation capacities and exchanges

The capacity for humanity to use science, technology and innovation to confront crises in transformative ways, and for science, technology and innovation to deliver for the public good, was clear during the pandemic. The potential for science, technology and innovation to be applied to the Sustainable Development Goals is vastly untapped, and institutional and other barriers that stand in the way of science, technology and innovation progress must be recognized and lowered.

Increasing funding for Goals-related research and innovation on underlying social issues, social policy and grass-roots innovations, in particular in low-income countries, would provide the data, evidence and analytical tools to better inform actions for the Goals. Access to knowledge, technology and opportunities to contribute to science, technology and innovation development must be improved, including through strengthened technology transfer. Creative solutions for removing paywalls and sharing knowledge need to be scaled up, and public-private partnerships should boost digital infrastructure investments, but Governments have to ensure that appropriate regulatory frameworks are in place. Applying science to solve complex interlinked challenges calls for cross-disciplinary collaboration. A strong science-policy-society interface can build trust in science and evidence, as emphasized in the 2023 Global Sustainable Development Report. Trust in the science behind COVID-19 vaccines and climate change, for example, needs to be built through open and inclusive deliberations for individuals to use technology solutions and change behaviour.

Priority actions:

 Strengthen the science-policy-society interface to enable the application of science, technology and innovation for the achievement of the Goals by taking all steps to strengthen the linkages between the scientific community and policymakers.

 Build trust in scientific knowledge by ensuring that information is broadcast with integrity, including by instituting regulatory mechanisms and codes of conduct that promote integrity in public information, as recommended by Our Common Agenda.

 Establish more efficient and effective technology transfer mechanisms and strengthen existing mechanisms such as the Technology Facilitation Mechanism, while exploring new avenues for open science and open-source data.

 Increase funding for Goals-related research and innovation on underlying social issues and build capacity in all regions to contribute to and benefit from this research.

Maximize the contribution of multilateralism and the United Nations development system to support acceleration of the Sustainable Development Goals

The above sections of the present report have demonstrated the degree to which multilateralism can support national action to achieve the Goals. Our Common Agenda includes a wide range of recommendations to that end, many of which are already under way.

The preparations for the Summit of the Future in 2024 provide a critical opportunity to leverage multilateralism's capacity to support acceleration of the Goals and to sustain Goals-related progress by planning for and tackling emerging challenges and addressing gaps and weaknesses in the international architecture that are undermining efforts to achieve the 2030 Agenda. Further action in a number of areas in the context of the Summit of the Future – including a global digital compact, progress on reforms of the international financing architecture, measuring progress by going beyond GDP, ensuring that governance systems protect the rights of future generations and facilitate the active engagement of young people in decision-making, and transforming education to better prepare learners of all ages for the future – will further support acceleration of the Goals.

The United Nations development system is the strongest affirmation to people across the world of the commitment of the United Nations to the Sustainable Development Goals. In 2018, the General Assembly, in its resolution 72/279, embraced an ambitious reform of the United Nations development system to ensure that Member States had the transformative support required to advance their national Goals-related ambitions. At the midpoint of the Goals, the United Nations development system is unquestionably better positioned to support Member State action for delivery of the Goals. The new generation of United Nations country teams and the reinvigorated resident coordinator system are better aligning with national priorities, shifting to higher-scale programmes and policy support. Resident Coordinators are convening in unprecedented ways to help Governments harness means of implementation, in particular financing. Some foundational challenges remain, in particular the insufficient implementation of the funding compact, especially in relation to core and pooled funding; an underfunded and unsustainably funded resident coordinator system, continued challenges in mobilizing support on economic and financial issues, and insufficient integration from the regional to national levels. If the United Nations system is to step up in the second half of the Goals, then targeted and determined action is needed in these areas.

Priority actions:

 Commit to an ambitious outcome at the Summit of the Future in 2024 to further revitalize the multilateral system, fill gaps in global governance and boost implementation of the Goals.

 Commit to fully supporting the United Nations development system to improve delivery in support of Member States' efforts to drive transformation of the Goals for inclusivity and sustainability, including through delivery against the funding compact, capitalizing the Joint Sustainable Development Goals Fund by at least $1 billion by September 2024 and putting in place an effective model to fully and sustainably resource the resident coordinator system in 2024 and, in the interim, taking urgent action to plug gaps in the funding of the system.

IV. Looking ahead: towards a rescue plan for people and planet

The world has been rocked by a series of interlinked crises. Together, these have exposed fundamental shortcomings in the business-as-usual approaches to sustainability, including the vulnerability and fragility of progress, growing inequalities, the life-long impacts of adverse events, increasing threats of irreversible change, risks of ignoring interlinkages, and the geographically imbalanced distribution of global assets for achieving sustainable development.

Tepid responses will not suffice for the millions of people living in poverty and hunger, the women and girls with unequal opportunities, the communities facing climate disaster or the families fleeing conflict. We need a full-fledged rescue plan for people and planet.

There are no excuses not to be ambitious. Never before have we had such an abundance of knowledge, technology and resources to succeed in ending poverty and saving the planet. Never before have we carried such a responsibility to pivot to a bold set of actions.

At the SDG Summit, we must match that abundance and responsibility with global, national and local commitments to deliver the finance, galvanize the leadership and restore the trust that together will put us on course to achieve the Goals by 2030.

Visual summary

 **1 NO POVERTY**

END POVERTY IN ALL ITS FORMS EVERYWHERE

IF CURRENT TRENDS CONTINUE,

BY 2030

575 MILLION
PEOPLE WILL STILL BE LIVING IN EXTREME POVERTY

ONLY ONE THIRD
OF COUNTRIES WILL HAVE HALVED THEIR NATIONAL POVERTY LEVELS

IN RESPONSE TO THE COST-OF-LIVING CRISIS,

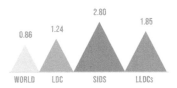

105 COUNTRIES
ANNOUNCED ALMOST 350 SOCIAL PROTECTION MEASURES IN THE PAST

12 MONTHS

(FEB. 2022 – FEB. 2023)

MANY OF THE

WORLD'S VULNERABLE POPULATION REMAIN UNCOVERED BY SOCIAL PROTECTION

 IN LOW-INCOME COUNTRIES, ONLY

8.5% OF CHILDREN

7.8% OF VULNERABLE PEOPLE

23.2% OF OLDER PERSONS

RECEIVED SOCIAL PROTECTION CASH BENEFITS

(2020)

LDCs, SIDS AND LLDCs
FACE HIGHER VULNERABILITY TO DISASTERS

AVERAGE ANNUAL NUMBER OF DEATHS OR MISSING PERSONS PER 100,000 POPULATION

(2012-2021)

| 0.86 | 1.24 | 2.80 | 1.85 |
| WORLD | LDC | SIDS | LLDCs |

WORLDWIDE, COUNTRIES HAVE INCREASED GOVERNMENT SPENDING ON ESSENTIAL SERVICES (EDUCATION, HEALTH AND SOCIAL PROTECTION) SINCE 2015

2015 — 47%

2021 — 53%

2 ZERO HUNGER

END HUNGER, ACHIEVE FOOD SECURITY AND IMPROVED NUTRITION AND PROMOTE SUSTAINABLE AGRICULTURE

ZERO HUNGER GOAL

AT RISK

MORE THAN **600 MILLION** PEOPLE WORLDWIDE ARE PROJECTED TO FACE HUNGER IN 2030

DESPITE DROPPING IN 2021,

HIGH FOOD PRICES CONTINUE TO PLAGUE MANY NATIONS

SHARE OF COUNTRIES EXPERIENCING MODERATELY TO ABNORMALLY HIGH FOOD PRICES:

48.1%

15.2%

21.5%

| 2015-2019 | 2020 | 2021 |

LITTLE TO NO PROGRESS

HAS BEEN MADE IN REDUCING ANAEMIA WORLDWIDE SINCE 2000

PREVALENCE OF ANAEMIA IN WOMEN AGED 15-49

HAS REMAINED STAGNANT AT AROUND 30%

1 IN 3 PEOPLE

WORLDWIDE STRUGGLE WITH MODERATE TO SEVERE FOOD INSECURITY

MALNUTRITION PERSISTS WORLDWIDE, JEOPARDIZING CHILDREN'S WELL-BEING AND FUTURE DEVELOPMENT

CHILDREN UNDER AGE-5 AFFECTED BY: (2022)

 STUNTING 148 MILLION

 WASTING 45 MILLION

 OVERWEIGHT 37 MILLION

ENSURE HEALTHY LIVES AND PROMOTE WELL-BEING FOR ALL AT ALL AGES

NOTABLE STRIDES HAVE BEEN MADE TOWARDS
IMPROVING GLOBAL HEALTH OUTCOMES

146 OUT OF 200
COUNTRIES OR AREAS **HAVE ALREADY MET OR ARE ON TRACK TO MEET** THE UNDER-5 MORTALITY TARGET

EFFECTIVE HIV TREATMENT HAS CUT GLOBAL AIDS-RELATED DEATHS BY
52% SINCE 2010

AT LEAST ONE NEGLECTED TROPICAL DISEASE **HAS BEEN ELIMINATED** IN
47 COUNTRIES

OUT-OF-POCKET PAYMENTS

FOR HEALTH PUSHED OR FURTHER PUSHED

381
MILLION PEOPLE
(4.9% OF POPULATION)

INTO EXTREME POVERTY

25 MILLION CHILDREN
MISSED OUT ON IMPORTANT ROUTINE IMMUNIZATIONS IN 2021

6 MILLION MORE
THAN IN 2019

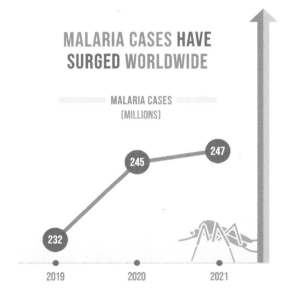

MALARIA CASES **HAVE SURGED WORLDWIDE**

MALARIA CASES
(MILLIONS)

232 — 2019
245 — 2020
247 — 2021

A WOMAN DIES EVERY
TWO MINUTES
FROM PREVENTABLE CAUSES RELATED TO PREGNANCY AND CHILDBIRTH
(2020)

4 QUALITY EDUCATION

ENSURE INCLUSIVE AND EQUITABLE QUALITY EDUCATION AND PROMOTE LIFELONG LEARNING OPPORTUNITIES FOR ALL

DESPITE SLOW PROGRESS,

THE WORLD IS FALLING FAR BEHIND IN ACHIEVING QUALITY EDUCATION

WITHOUT ADDITIONAL MEASURES, BY 2030:

84 MILLION
CHILDREN AND YOUTH WILL BE OUT OF SCHOOL

300 MILLION
STUDENTS WILL LACK BASIC NUMERACY/LITERACY SKILLS

ONLY 1 IN 6
COUNTRIES WILL ACHIEVE UNIVERSAL SECONDARY SCHOOL COMPLETION TARGET

THE PANDEMIC

CAUSED LEARNING LOSSES IN 4 IN 5 OF 104 COUNTRIES STUDIED

PRIMARY AND SECONDARY SCHOOL COMPLETION RATES ARE RISING, BUT THE PACE IS SLOW AND UNEVEN

COMPLETION RATES

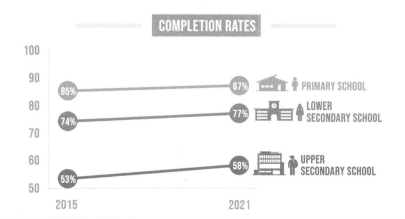

- 85% → 87% PRIMARY SCHOOL
- 74% → 77% LOWER SECONDARY SCHOOL
- 53% → 58% UPPER SECONDARY SCHOOL

2015 — 2021

LOW- AND LOWER-MIDDLE-INCOME COUNTRIES FACE A NEARLY

$100 BILLION ANNUAL FINANCING GAP TO REACH THEIR EDUCATION TARGETS

Visual summary

5 GENDER EQUALITY

ACHIEVE GENDER EQUALITY AND EMPOWER ALL WOMEN AND GIRLS

THE WORLD IS NOT ON TRACK TO ACHIEVE GENDER EQUALITY BY 2030

OUT OF GOAL 5 INDICATORS:

- 15.4 "ON TRACK"
- 23.1 AT A MODERATE DISTANCE
- 61.5 FAR OR VERY FAR OFF TRACK

············ AT THE CURRENT RATE, IT WILL TAKE ············

 300 YEARS TO END CHILD MARRIAGE

 286 YEARS TO CLOSE GAPS IN LEGAL PROTECTION AND REMOVE DISCRIMINATORY LAWS

140 YEARS TO ACHIEVE EQUAL REPRESENTATION IN LEADERSHIP IN THE WORKPLACE

LEGISLATED GENDER QUOTAS ARE EFFECTIVE TO ACHIEVE EQUALITY IN POLITICS

WOMEN'S REPRESENTATION IN PARLIAMENT
(2022)

30.9% COUNTRIES APPLYING QUOTAS

21.2% COUNTRIES WITHOUT QUOTAS

NEARLY HALF OF MARRIED WOMEN LACK DECISION-MAKING POWER OVER THEIR SEXUAL AND REPRODUCTIVE HEALTH AND RIGHTS

1 IN 5 YOUNG WOMEN

············ **ARE MARRIED** ············
BEFORE THEIR 18TH BIRTHDAY

SAFE DRINKING WATER, SANITATION AND HYGIENE

STILL OUT OF REACH

FOR BILLIONS

IN 2022

2.2 BILLION PEOPLE

LACKED SAFELY MANAGED DRINKING WATER

3.5 BILLION PEOPLE

LACKED SAFELY MANAGED SANITATION

2.2 BILLION PEOPLE

LACKED BASIC HAND WASHING FACILITIES

TO MEET 2030 TARGETS, PACE OF PROGRESS WILL HAVE TO ACCELERATE

6x
DRINKING WATER

5x
FOR SANITATION

3x
HYGIENE

2.4 BILLION PEOPLE
LIVE IN
WATER-STRESSED COUNTRIES
(2020)

81% OF SPECIES

DEPENDENT ON INLAND WETLANDS HAVE **DECLINED** SINCE 1970

INTEGRATED WATER-RESOURCES-MANAGEMENT IMPLEMENTATION **NEEDS ACCELERATION**

NUMBER OF COUNTRIES PER PROGRESS LEVEL

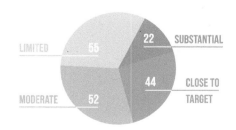

LIMITED 55
SUBSTANTIAL 22
CLOSE TO TARGET 44
MODERATE 52

ENSURE ACCESS TO AFFORDABLE, RELIABLE, SUSTAINABLE AND MODERN ENERGY FOR ALL

LIGHTS OUT:
675 MILLION PEOPLE
STILL LIVE IN THE DARK

4 IN 5 OF THEM ARE IN SUB-SAHARAN AFRICA
(2021)

IF CURRENT TRENDS CONTINUE,

1 IN 4 PEOPLE WILL STILL USE UNSAFE AND INEFFICIENT COOKING SYSTEMS BY 2030

ENERGY EFFICIENCY IMPROVEMENT MUST MORE THAN DOUBLE ITS PACE

ANNUAL ENERGY-INTENSITY IMPROVEMENT RATE

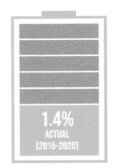

1.4%
ACTUAL
(2015-2020)

3.4%
NEEDED
(2020-2030)

INTERNATIONAL PUBLIC FINANCING FOR CLEAN ENERGY FOR DEVELOPING COUNTRIES CONTINUES TO DECLINE

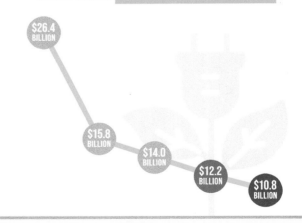

$26.4 BILLION
$15.8 BILLION
$14.0 BILLION
$12.2 BILLION
$10.8 BILLION

2017   2018   2019   2020   2021

MODERN RENEWABLES POWER NEARLY 30% OF ELECTRICITY, BUT REMAIN LOW IN HEATING AND TRANSPORT (2020)

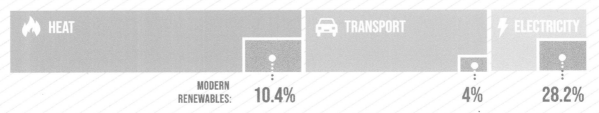

HEAT	TRANSPORT	ELECTRICITY
MODERN RENEWABLES: 10.4%	4%	28.2%

PROMOTE SUSTAINED, INCLUSIVE AND SUSTAINABLE ECONOMIC GROWTH, FULL AND PRODUCTIVE EMPLOYMENT AND DECENT WORK FOR ALL

GLOBAL ECONOMIC RECOVERY CONTINUES, BUT ON A SLOW TRAJECTORY

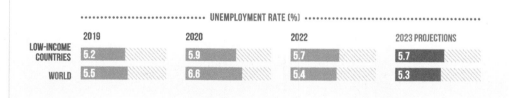

GLOBAL ANNUAL GROWTH RATE OF REAL GDP PER CAPITA (%)

2020 : −4.1
2021 : 5.2
2022 : 2.2
2023 PROJECTION : 1.4
2024 PROJECTION : 1.6

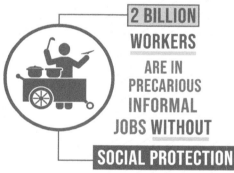

2 BILLION WORKERS ARE IN PRECARIOUS INFORMAL JOBS WITHOUT **SOCIAL PROTECTION**

(2022)

GLOBAL UNEMPLOYMENT IS EXPECTED TO FALL BELOW PRE-PANDEMIC LEVELS, BUT NOT IN LOW-INCOME COUNTRIES

UNEMPLOYMENT RATE (%)

	2019	2020	2022	2023 PROJECTIONS
LOW-INCOME COUNTRIES	5.2	5.9	5.7	5.7
WORLD	5.5	6.6	5.4	5.3

---

1 IN 4 YOUNG PEOPLE

ARE NOT IN EDUCATION, EMPLOYMENT OR TRAINING,

WITH YOUNG WOMEN MORE THAN **TWICE AS LIKELY** AS YOUNG MEN TO BE IN THIS SITUATION

(2022)

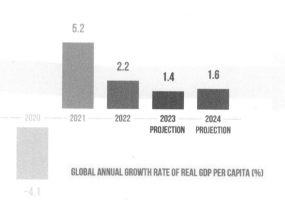

DURING THE PANDEMIC, 4 IN 10 ADULTS IN LOW- AND MIDDLE-INCOME COUNTRIES OPENED THEIR FIRST BANK ACCOUNT

9 INDUSTRY, INNOVATION AND INFRASTRUCTURE

BUILD RESILIENT INFRASTRUCTURE, PROMOTE INCLUSIVE AND SUSTAINABLE INDUSTRIALIZATION AND FOSTER INNOVATION

GLOBAL MANUFACTURING
GROWTH SLOWED FROM

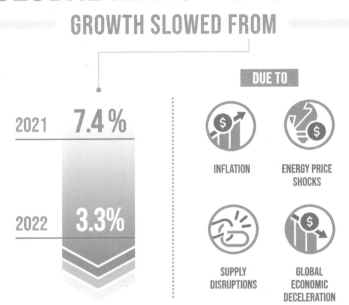

2021 **7.4%**

2022 **3.3%**

DUE TO

INFLATION

ENERGY PRICE SHOCKS

SUPPLY DISRUPTIONS

GLOBAL ECONOMIC DECELERATION

ENERGY-RELATED CO_2 EMISSIONS

REACHED

36.8 BILLION

METRIC TONS IN 2022

A RECORD HIGH

LDCs ARE LIKELY TO MISS THEIR 2030 TARGET OF DOUBLING MANUFACTURING SHARE OF GDP

MANUFACTURING VALUE AS A SHARE OF GDP IN LDCs

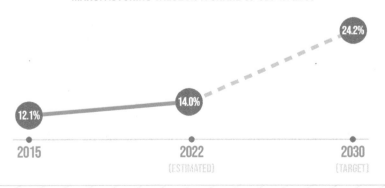

12.1% 2015 — 14.0% 2022 (ESTIMATED) — 24.2% 2030 (TARGET)

MEDIUM-HIGH AND HIGH-TECHNOLOGY INDUSTRIES EXPERIENCED
STRONG GROWTH IN 2022
BUT WITH REGIONAL VARIATION

SHARE IN TOTAL MANUFACTURING

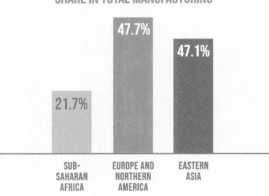

21.7% SUB-SAHARAN AFRICA | 47.7% EUROPE AND NORTHERN AMERICA | 47.1% EASTERN ASIA

82% SUB-SAHARAN AFRICA

68% OCEANIA* (*EXCLUDING AUSTRALIA AND NEW ZEALAND)

95% OF THE WORLD HAS MOBILE BROADBAND ACCESS (3G OR HIGHER) (2022)

BUT COVERAGE IS ONLY 82% IN SUB-SAHARAN AFRICA AND 68% IN OCEANIA*

10 REDUCED INEQUALITIES

REDUCE INEQUALITY WITHIN AND AMONG COUNTRIES

COVID-19 TRIGGERS THE LARGEST INCREASE IN BETWEEN-COUNTRY INEQUALITY IN THREE DECADES,

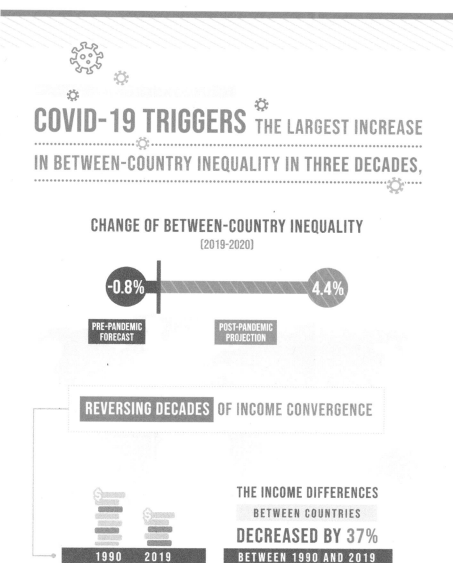

CHANGE OF BETWEEN-COUNTRY INEQUALITY
(2019-2020)

-0.8%
4.4%

PRE-PANDEMIC FORECAST

POST-PANDEMIC PROJECTION

REVERSING DECADES OF INCOME CONVERGENCE

THE INCOME DIFFERENCES
BETWEEN COUNTRIES
DECREASED BY 37%

1990   2019

BETWEEN 1990 AND 2019

IN 2022,
REFUGEE NUMBERS HIT A RECORD HIGH OF

34.6 MILLION

AMONG THEM WERE:
● CHILDREN: 41%

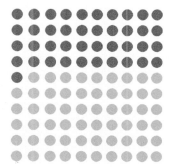

GLOBALLY,
WOMEN ARE TWICE AS LIKELY AS MEN
TO REPORT EXPERIENCING DISCRIMINATION
BASED ON THEIR SEX

THE TRAGIC LOSS OF NEARLY 7,000 LIVES ALONG MIGRATORY ROUTES IN 2022

UNDERSCORES THE PRESSING NEED FOR
IMMEDIATE ACTION TO ENSURE SAFE MIGRATION

MAKE CITIES AND HUMAN SETTLEMENTS INCLUSIVE, SAFE, RESILIENT AND SUSTAINABLE

SLUMS ON THE RISE

1.1 BILLION URBAN RESIDENTS ARE LIVING IN SLUMS (2020)

2 BILLION MORE ARE EXPECTED IN THE NEXT 30 YEARS

GLOBALLY, ONLY

ONE IN TWO
URBAN RESIDENTS HAVE CONVENIENT ACCESS TO

PUBLIC TRANSPORT

[2022]

AIR POLLUTION IS NO LONGER AN EXCLUSIVELY URBAN PROBLEM

TOWNS EXPERIENCE **POORER AIR QUALITY**

THAN CITIES IN EASTERN AND SOUTH-EASTERN ASIA (2019)

IN THE DEVELOPING WORLD

1 BILLION PEOPLE LACK ACCESS TO **ALL-WEATHER ROADS** (2022)

GLOBALLY,

3 IN 4 CITIES

HAVE **LESS THAN 20%** OF THEIR AREA DEDICATED TO PUBLIC SPACES AND STREETS

MUCH LOWER THAN THE TARGET OF 45-50% [2020]

ENSURE SUSTAINABLE CONSUMPTION AND PRODUCTION PATTERNS

HIGH-INCOME COUNTRIES

LEAVE A **LARGER ENVIRONMENTAL FOOTPRINT** COMPARED TO

LOW-INCOME COUNTRIES

MATERIAL FOOTPRINT PER CAPITA IN HIGH-INCOME COUNTRIES IS

10 TIMES THAT OF LOW-INCOME COUNTRIES

MATERIAL FOOTPRINT PER CAPITA

24 METRIC TONS

2.5 METRIC TONS

(2019)

HIGH-INCOME COUNTRIES

LOW-INCOME COUNTRIES

SUSTAINABILITY PATHWAY

62 COUNTRIES + EU
— INTRODUCED —

485 POLICIES

FOR SUSTAINABLE CONSUMPTION AND PRODUCTION SHIFTS
(2019-2022)

DESPITE CALLS FOR

A PHASE-OUT

FOSSIL FUEL SUBSIDIES RETURN AND NEARLY DOUBLED, TRIGGERED BY **GLOBAL CRISES**

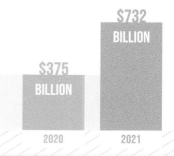

$732 BILLION

$375 BILLION

2020

2021

ON AVERAGE, **EACH PERSON** WASTES

120 KILOGRAMS

OF FOOD **PER YEAR**

COMPANY SUSTAINABILITY REPORTING HAS **TRIPLED** SINCE 2016

TAKE URGENT ACTION TO COMBAT CLIMATE CHANGE AND ITS IMPACTS

EARTH'S TIPPING POINT

STANDING AT THE BRINK OF CLIMATE CALAMITY

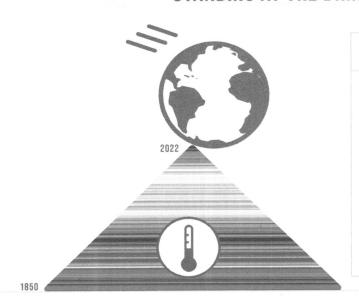

2022

1850

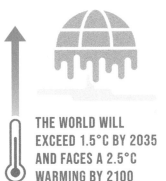

WHERE WE ARE

THE WORLD WILL EXCEED 1.5°C BY 2035 AND FACES A 2.5°C WARMING BY 2100

WHAT WE NEED

DEEP, RAPID AND SUSTAINED GHG EMISSION REDUCTIONS BY 43% BY 2030 AND TO NET ZERO BY 2050

BILLIONS TO TRILLIONS:

GLOBAL CLIMATE FINANCE FLOWS REACHED AN ANNUAL AVERAGE OF $803 BILLION IN 2019–2020

HOWEVER, DEVELOPING COUNTRIES REQUIRE NEARLY $6 TRILLION BY 2030

$6 TRILLION

$803 BILLION

2019–2020 (ANNUAL AVERAGE)

2030

THE RATE OF SEA-LEVEL RISE HAS **DOUBLED** IN THE LAST DECADE

HIGHLY VULNERABLE REGIONS

EXPERIENCE **15X HIGHER MORTALITY RATES** FROM DISASTERS

COMPARED TO VERY LOW VULNERABILITY REGIONS (2010–2020)

PRESERVE THE BLUE, PROTECT THE EARTH:
URGENT ACTIONS NEEDED TO SAFEGUARD THE PLANET'S LARGEST ECOSYSTEM

OCEAN EMERGENCY

COASTAL EUTROPHICATION:	OCEAN ACIDIFICATION:	OCEAN WARMING:	PLASTIC POLLUTION:	OVER-FISHING:
CAUSING ALGAL BLOOMS AND DEAD ZONES	30% HIGHER THAN IN PRE-INDUSTRIAL TIMES	SEA-LEVEL RISE AND AFFECTING MARINE ECOSYSTEMS	17 MILLION METRIC TONS IN 2021– 2-3X MORE BY 2040	MORE THAN A THIRD OF GLOBAL FISH STOCKS ARE OVERFISHED

CITIZEN SCIENCE BEACH CLEAN-UPS
- SHED LIGHT ON THE MAGNITUDE OF
OCEAN PLASTIC POLLUTION

SUFFOCATING SEAS
- COASTAL EUTROPHICATION TRIGGERS
CRUSTACEAN WALKOUTS

OCEAN ACIDIFICATION
REPORTING STATIONS HAVE TRIPLED WORLDWIDE

2021: 178 STATIONS
2022: 308 STATIONS
2023: 539 STATIONS

1 IN 5 FISH CAUGHT
ORIGINATES FROM ILLEGAL, UNREPORTED AND UNREGULATED FISHING

PROTECT, RESTORE AND PROMOTE SUSTAINABLE USE OF TERRESTRIAL ECOSYSTEMS, SUSTAINABLY MANAGE FORESTS, COMBAT DESERTIFICATION, AND HALT AND REVERSE LAND DEGRADATION AND HALT BIODIVERSITY LOSS

A FUNDAMENTAL SHIFT IN HUMANITY'S RELATIONSHIP WITH NATURE IS ESSENTIAL

ESCALATING

FOREST LOSSES

LAND DEGRADATION

SPECIES EXTINCTION

POSE SEVERE THREATS TO PEOPLE AND THE PLANET

100 MILLION HECTARES OF HEALTHY AND PRODUCTIVE LAND WAS DEGRADED EVERY YEAR

FROM 2015–2019

EQUIVALENT TO 2X THE SIZE OF GREENLAND

THE WORLD IS CURRENTLY FACING THE **LARGEST SPECIES EXTINCTION** EVENT SINCE THE DINOSAUR AGE

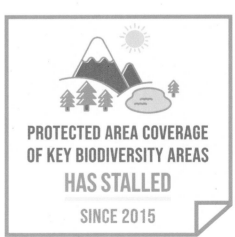

PROTECTED AREA COVERAGE OF KEY BIODIVERSITY AREAS HAS STALLED

SINCE 2015

THE KUNMING-MONTREAL GLOBAL BIODIVERSITY FRAMEWORK
PROVIDES RENEWED IMPETUS FOR CONSERVING TERRESTRIAL ECOSYSTEMS, WITH:

 4 OUTCOME-ORIENTED GOALS BY 2050

 23 TARGETS BY 2030

PROMOTE PEACEFUL AND INCLUSIVE SOCIETIES FOR SUSTAINABLE DEVELOPMENT, PROVIDE ACCESS TO JUSTICE FOR ALL AND BUILD EFFECTIVE, ACCOUNTABLE AND INCLUSIVE INSTITUTIONS AT ALL LEVELS

STEEP RISE IN

CONFLICT-RELATED CIVILIAN DEATHS

WITH AN OVER **50% SURGE** IN 2022, FUELED BY THE **WAR IN UKRAINE**

2021 SAW

THE HIGHEST NUMBER OF INTENTIONAL HOMICIDES IN 20 YEARS

458,000 LIVES LOST

9 IN 10 VICTIMS WERE MALE

MORE THAN

108.4 MILLION PEOPLE

HAD BEEN FORCIBLY DISPLACED WORLDWIDE AS OF END-2022

2.5X THE NUMBER A DECADE AGO

NEARLY **200,000**

TRAFFICKING VICTIMS

WERE DETECTED WORLDWIDE BETWEEN 2017 AND 2020

BUT MANY MORE LIKELY REMAINED **UNDETECTED**

YOUTH FACE UNDERREPRESENTATION IN POLITICS,
HINDERING THEIR PARTICIPATION IN DECISION-MAKING PROCESSES

 **30** ——————
GLOBAL MEDIAN AGE

 **51** ——————
AVERAGE AGE OF MEMBERS OF PARLIAMENT

MANY DEVELOPING COUNTRIES ARE FACING A DEBT CRISIS

AS OF NOVEMBER 2022,

69

DEBT DISTRESSED   37   THE WORLD'S POOREST COUNTRIES

37 OUT OF 69
OF THE WORLD'S POOREST COUNTRIES WERE IN DEBT DISTRESS OR AT HIGH RISK OF IT

THE SHARE OF EXPORTS FROM **LDCs** IN GLOBAL MERCHANDISE TRADE

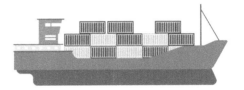

HAS STAGNATED AT AROUND **1%**

SINCE 2011

NET ODA REACHED **$206 BILLION** IN 2022, UP 15.3% FROM 2021

MAINLY OWING TO SPENDING ON REFUGEES IN DONOR COUNTRIES AND AID TO UKRAINE

NET ODA REACHED 0.37% OF GNI, STILL BELOW THE TARGET OF 0.7%

2 IN 3 PEOPLE USED THE INTERNET
IN 2022

259 MILLION MORE MALE THAN FEMALE USERS

ODA FUNDING FOR DATA

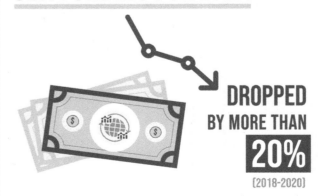

DROPPED BY MORE THAN **20%**
(2018-2020)

Note to the reader

Global indicator framework for the follow-up and review of the Sustainable Development Goals

The information presented in this report is based on the latest available data (as of June 2023) on selected indicators in the global indicator framework[1] for the Sustainable Development Goals. The global indicator framework is used to review progress at the global level and was developed by the Inter-Agency and Expert Group on SDG Indicators (IAEG-SDGs) and adopted by the General Assembly on 6 July 2017 (see resolution 71/313, annex). The choice of indicators used in the report does not represent a prioritization of targets, since all goals and targets are equally important.

Data sources

The values for most of the indicators presented in the report are regional and/or subregional aggregates. In general, the figures are weighted averages, using the reference population as a weight, of national data produced by national statistical systems and calculated by international agencies with specialized mandates. The national data are often adjusted for comparability and, where lacking, are estimated. As decided by the United Nations Statistical Commission and in accordance with Economic and Social Council resolution 2006/6, estimates used to compile the global indicators should be produced in full consultation with national statistical authorities. The criteria and mechanisms for validation by national statistical authorities are outlined in the report of the IAEG-SDGs[2] and were endorsed by the Statistical Commission at its fiftieth session.[3]

Although the aggregate figures presented here are a convenient way to track progress, the situation of individual countries within a given region, and across population groups and geographical areas within a country, may vary significantly from regional averages. Presenting aggregate figures for all regions also obscures another reality: the lack, in many parts of the world, of adequate data to assess national trends and to inform and monitor the implementation of development policies.

A database of available global, regional and country data and metadata for the SDG indicators is maintained by the United Nations Statistics Division at https://unstats.un.org/sdgs. Owing to the emergence of new data and revised methodologies, data series presented in this report may not be comparable with previous data series.

Regional groupings

This report presents data on progress made towards achieving the SDGs worldwide and by various regional groups. The country groupings are based on the geographic regions defined in the Standard Country or Area Codes for Statistical Use (known as M49)[4] of the United Nations Statistics Division. The geographic regions are shown on the map on the right. For the purpose of presentation, some of the M49 regions have been combined.

The use of geographic regions as the basis for country groupings is a major change from *The Sustainable Development Goals Report 2016* and the progress reports on the Millennium Development Goals. Previously, data were presented for countries in "developed" and "developing" regions, which were further broken down into geographic subregions. Although there is no established convention for the designation of "developed" and "developing" countries or areas in the United Nations system, data for some indicators in this report are still being presented for developed and developing regions and countries for the purpose of statistical analysis only, and are based on the practice employed by the international agencies that provided the data.[5]

The text and figures present, to the extent possible, data for least developed countries, landlocked developing countries and small island developing States, which are country groups requiring special attention.

A complete list of countries included in each region and subregion and country group is available at https://unstats.un.org/sdgs/indicators/regional-groups/.

The term "country" used in this report also refers, as appropriate, to territories and areas. The designations employed and the presentation of the material in this report do not imply the expression of any opinion whatsoever on the part of the United Nations Secretariat concerning the legal status of any country, territory, city or area or of its authorities, or concerning the delimitation of its frontiers or boundaries.

- ● Sub-Saharan Africa
- ● Northern Africa and Western Asia
- ● Eastern and South-Eastern Asia
- ● Central and Southern Asia
- ● Oceania*
- ● Europe and Northern America
- ● Latin America and the Caribbean
- ● Australia and New Zealand

Notes: • Oceania* refers to Oceania excluding Australia and New Zealand, throughout the publication.

• The boundaries and names shown and the designations used on this and other maps throughout this publication do not imply official endorsement or acceptance by the United Nations.

---

1 The complete list of indicators is available at https://unstats.un.org/sdgs/indicators/indicators-list/.
2 See the "Report of the Inter-Agency and Expert Group on Sustainable Development Goal Indicators" (E/CN.3/2019/2), annex I.
3 See Report of the Statistical Commission on its fiftieth session (E/2019/24-E/CN.3/2019/34).
4 Full details of the M49 standard can be found on the Statistics Division website at https://unstats.un.org/unsd/methodology/m49.
5 The discussion note, "Update of the regional groupings for the SDG report and database", of 31 October 2016 describes the details of this change and is available at https://unstats.un.org/sdgs/indicators/regional-groups.

Photo credits:
Cover © UNICEF/Mark Naftalin
Page 4 © WHO/Yoshi Shimizu
Page 7 © UNDP Kenya/Allan Gichigi
Page 12 © World Bank/Dominic Chavez
Page 14 © WFP/Derrick Botchway
Page 16 © UNICEF/Radoslaw Czajkowskito
Page 20 © UNICEF/Ali Haj Suleiman
Page 22 © UN Women/Johis Alarcón
Page 24 © UNICEF/Mulugaeta Ayene
Page 26 © UNDP Lebanon/Rana Sweidan
Page 28 © ILO/Ahmad Al-Basha/Gabreez
Page 30 © UNDP Bhutan/Dechen Wangmo
Page 32 © UNICEF
Page 34 © World Bank/Yayo López
Page 36 © UNEP/Ollivier Girard
Page 38 © UNICEF/Asad Zaidi
Page 40 © UNDP Timor-Leste/Yuichi Ishida
Page 42 © UNEP/Braunosarus Studios
Page 44 © UNDP Somalia/Fadhaye
Page 46 © UN Photo/Rick Bajornas
Page 49 © UNDP Peru/Mónica Suárez Galindo
Page 50 © UN Photo/Martine Perret
Page 55 © UNDP Bolivia

Map credits: Maps on pages 14, 24, 25 and 42 are from the United Nations Department of Economic and Social Affairs Statistics Division.
Mapping data are provided by the United Nations Geospatial Information Section.
Design (report and Visual summary infographics on pages 58–74):
Mackenzie Crone and Dewi Glanville

Additional report design, graphics design, copy-editing, typesetting and proofreading:
Content Services Unit/Department for General Assembly and Conference Management
Editor: Jennifer Ross

ISBN: 978-92-1-101460-0
e-ISBN: 978-92-1-002492-1
ISSN: 2518-3915
e-ISSN: 251-3958
Sales No. E.23.I.4